My
Social Media
for Seniors

Michael Miller

Real Possibilities

800 East 96th Street

Indianapoli

My Social Media for Seniors

Copyright © 2016 by Pearson Education, Inc.

ISBN-13: 978-0-7897-5570-4

ISBN-10: 0-7897-5570-x

Library of Congress Control Number: 2015950787

Printed in the United States of America

First Printing: November 2015

Trademarks

Warning and Disclaimer

Special Sales

For information about buying this title in bulk quantities, or for special sales opportunities (which may include electronic versions; custom cover designs; and content particular to your business, training goals, marketing focus, or branding interests), please contact our corporate sales department at corpsales@pearsoned.com or (800) 382-3419.

For government sales inquiries, please contact governmentsales@pearsoned.com.

For questions about sales outside the U.S., please contact international@pearsoned.com.

Editor-in-Chief
Greg Weigand

Acquisitions Editor
Michelle Newcomb

Marketing Manager
Dan Powell

Director, AARP Books
Jodi Lipson

Development Editor
Brandon Cackowski-Schnell

Managing Editor
Sandra Schroeder

Senior Project Editor
Tonya Simpson

Copy Editor
Anne Goebel

Indexer
Johnna Vanhoose Dinse

Proofreader
Kathy Ruiz

Technical Editor
Jeri Usbay

Editorial Assistant
Cindy Teeters

Cover Designer
Mark Shirar

Compositor
Mary Sudul

Contents at a Glance

Table of Contents

3   Using Social Media—Safely and Privately   35

4   Comparing the Most Popular Social Media   47

About the Author

Michael Miller is a prolific and popular writer of more than 150 nonfiction books, known for his ability to explain complex topics to everyday readers. He writes about a variety of topics, including technology, business, and music. His best-selling books for Que include *My Facebook for Seniors, My Windows 10 Computer for Seniors, My Samsung Galaxy S6 for Seniors, My Google Chromebook, Easy Computer Basics,* and *Computer Basics: Absolute Beginner's Guide.* Worldwide, his books have sold more than 1 million copies.

Find out more at the author's website: **www.millerwriter.com**

Follow the author on Twitter: **@molehillgroup**

About AARP and AARP TEK

AARP is a nonprofit, nonpartisan organization, with a membership of nearly 38 million, that helps people turn their goals and dreams into *real possibilities*™, strengthens communities, and fights for the issues that matter most to families such as healthcare, employment and income security, retirement planning, affordable utilities, and protection from financial abuse. Learn more at aarp.org.

The AARP TEK (Technology Education & Knowledge) program aims to accelerate AARP's mission of turning dreams into *real possibilities*™ by providing step-by-step lessons in a variety of formats to accommodate different learning styles, levels of experience, and interests. Expertly guided hands-on workshops delivered in communities nationwide help instill confidence and enrich lives of the 50+ by equipping them with skills for staying connected to the people and passions in their lives. Lessons are taught on touchscreen tablets and smartphones—common tools for connection, education, entertainment, and productivity. For self-paced lessons, videos, articles, and other resources, visit aarptek.org.

Dedication

To Lloyd Short, my old friend and mentor, enjoy your final role.

Acknowledgments

Thanks to all the folks at Que who helped turn this manuscript into a book, including Michelle Newcomb, Greg Wiegand, Brandon Cackowski-Schnell, Anne Goebel, Tonya Simpson, and technical editor Jeri Usbay. Thanks also to the good folks at AARP for supporting this and other books I've written.

Note: Most of the individuals pictured throughout this book are of the author himself, as well as friends and relatives (and sometimes pets). Some names and personal information are fictitious.

We Want to Hear from You!

As the reader of this book, *you* are our most important critic and commentator. We value your opinion and want to know what we're doing right, what we could do better, what areas you'd like to see us publish in, and any other words of wisdom you're willing to pass our way.

We welcome your comments. You can email or write to let us know what you did or didn't like about this book—as well as what we can do to make our books better.

Please note that we cannot help you with technical problems related to the topic of this book.

When you write, please be sure to include this book's title and author as well as your name and email address. We will carefully review your comments and share them with the author and editors who worked on the book.

Email: feedback@quepublishing.com

Mail: Que Publishing
ATTN: Reader Feedback
800 East 96th Street
Indianapolis, IN 46240 USA

Reader Services

Visit our website and register this book at quepublishing.com/register for convenient access to any updates, downloads, or errata that might be available for this book.

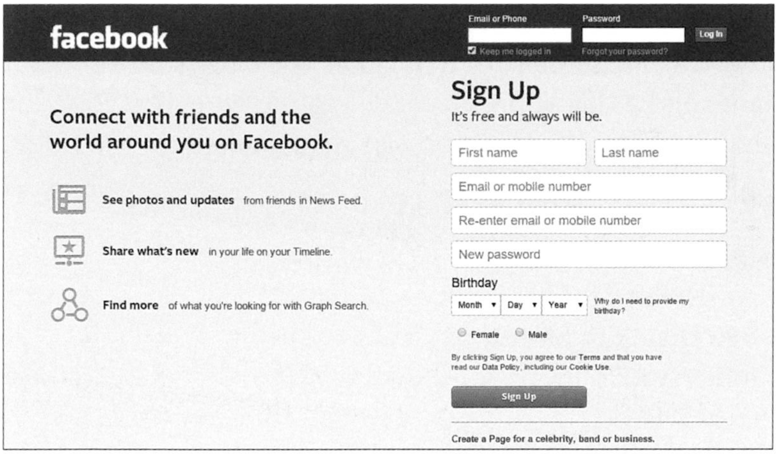

facebook

Email or Phone   Password

☑ Keep me logged in   Forgot your password?   Log In

Connect with friends and the world around you on Facebook.

See photos and updates from friends in News Feed.

Share what's new in your life on your Timeline.

Find more of what you're looking for with Graph Search.

Sign Up

It's free and always will be.

First name | Last name

Email or mobile number

Re-enter email or mobile number

New password

Birthday

Month ▼ | Day ▼ | Year ▼   Why do I need to provide my birthday?

○ Female   ○ Male

By clicking Sign Up, you agree to our Terms and that you have read our Data Policy, including our Cookie Use.

Sign Up

Create a Page for a celebrity, band or business.

In this chapter, you learn all about social media—what it is, how it works, and why you might want to use it.

1

What Social Media Is— and Why We Use It

You've heard people talking about this thing called *social media*. Chances are, some of your friends, family, and colleagues use Facebook, LinkedIn, or Pinterest or some similar site. You may even have your own Facebook account, even if you don't use it much.

The term "social media" might sound complicated or technical or even a little confusing. Don't worry; it isn't. In reality, social media such as Facebook and Pinterest help you connect with your family and friends. It's a new way to communicate with people you know and people you might like to know. And it's all done on your computer or smartphone or tablet, over the Internet.

Understanding Social Media

What exactly is—or is it *are*?—social media? There are lots of different definitions, but they all hinge on that one word: *social*.

Defining Social Media

Merriam-Webster defines social media as "forms of electronic communication… through which users create online communities to share information, ideas, personal messages, and other content…"

That's pretty technical. I like to think of social media as websites or services that host a community of users, and make it easy for those users to communicate with one another using their computers, smartphones, or tablets. That communication can involve sharing messages and information, as well as pictures and videos. It's all about being social, and encouraging social interactions.

In most instances, these social interactions come in the form of *posts* or *status updates*. These are short messages that are posted for public viewing by all of that person's friends on the site.

A status update posted on Facebook

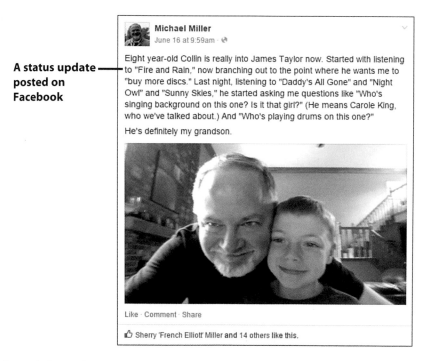

A social media post can be a text-only message or, depending on the site, include photographs, videos, and links to web pages. Whatever form the media takes, it's all about sharing things—socially.

What's in a Name?

What some people call *social media* others call *social networks*. Both names refer to the same thing. That is, a social network is social media, and vice versa. So don't get hung up on the name.

How Social Media Works

For most people, social media is all about communicating and staying in touch with one another. It's the 21st-century way to let people know what you're up to—and to find out what everyone else is up to as well.

Of course, people have been communicating and sharing things long before we ever heard of the Internet. We just used different media than we use today.

In the old, old days, the only way you found out about what was going on was for someone to write you a letter. That probably sounds quaint today, as letter writing is somewhat out of fashion. But I'm guessing you're old enough to have written a few letters in your time, so you know what I'm talking about.

Ah, the joys of receiving a letter from an old friend! I miss seeing a friend's address in the top left corner, opening the envelope, and savoring the words within. Of course, most friends didn't write that often; writing was a lot of work, so you saved up your thoughts and experiences until you had a full letter's worth. But, man, it was great to read what your friends had been doing. It almost made the wait worthwhile.

That was then and this is now. Today, nobody has the time or the patience or the attention span to write or read long letters. At some point back in the 1990s, email replaced the written letter as our primary means of correspondence. That wasn't necessarily a bad thing; emails were shorter than written letters, but you got them immediately—and you could respond to them immediately, too. With the Internet age came this faster and more direct form of communication, and we adapted to it.

For younger people today, however, email is old hat. It's too slow and takes too much time. (They'd never have tolerated the age of the written letter…) Instead, most people nowadays prefer immediate communication, primarily (if not exclusively) via text messages on their phones and mobile devices.

The problem with text messages is that they're not centralized. If you're texting with a dozen friends, that's a dozen different "feeds" of information you have to keep track of. There's no central repository where you can read all your friends' messages in one place.

This is where social media comes in. Instead of writing a dozen (or a hundred) different letters or emails or texts to each of your friends telling them that you just bought a new dress (or car or house or whatever), you write a single post that those dozen (or hundred) different people can then read. Something happens, you write about it, it gets posted on the social networking site, and everyone you know reads about it. It takes all the work out of keeping your friends up to date on what you're doing.

Of course, it works in the other direction, too. Instead of waiting for letters or emails or text messages from each of your friends, you just log onto your friendly local social media site. There you find a feed of updates from everyone you know. Read the feed and you're instantly updated on what everyone is up to. That makes it really easy to keep in touch.

Now, social media lets you do a lot more than just exchange status updates, but that's the most common activity and the reason most of us do the social media thing. Communications to and from all your friends, all in one place, all done from your personal computer or smartphone or tablet. It's like communications central for everyone you know—close friends or otherwise.

Building Social Communities

When you share your thoughts and interests via social media, you help to create online communities. To help facilitate this community building, many social media networks let you do more than exchange simple status updates. Depending on the social network, you may find some or all of the following features:

- **Private communications.** This can take the form of one-to-one private messaging, proprietary email service, and even live text messaging.

- **Video chat.** This is true face-to-face communications, in real time—assuming both parties have cameras on their personal computers (PCs) or smartphones, of course.

- **Groups and forums.** These are like online clubs built around specific areas of interest. You can find groups for hobbies like woodworking or quilting, for topics like politics or sports, for just about anything you can think of. There are even groups devoted to specific companies, schools, and entertainers. (Groups for entertainers are more like fan clubs than anything else.)

- **Photo and video sharing.** That's right, many social networks let you upload your pictures and movies and share them with all your friends on the network. It's the 21st-century way of sharing your photos—no slides or prints necessary.

- **Social games.** If you have too much free time on your hands, most social networks include fun games you can play with other members. Some of these games are quite addicting.

There's a bit more than even all this, including event scheduling and the like, but you get the general idea. Social media *are* online communities, and offer many of the same activities that you'd find in real-world communities.

A Short History of Social Media

The social media that we know today have been around for only about a decade—although their core features have existed since the earliest days of the Internet.

If you're old enough to remember the earliest PCs back in the 1970s and 1980s, you may remember pre-Internet communications in the form of dial-up computer networks (such as CompuServe, Prodigy, and America Online), bulletin board systems (BBSs), and other simple online discussion forums. Well, these early online services served much the same function as do today's social media, offering topic-based discussion forums and chat rooms, just like Facebook and LinkedIn do today. What they didn't offer was a way to follow friends on the site, or to publicly share status updates. But the seeds of today's social media were there.

Other components of modern social media developed after the rise of the public Internet and the World Wide Web. For example, numerous topic-based website communities, like iVillage, Epicurious, and Classmates.com, arose in the mid-1990s. Personal blogs, which let users post short articles of information and opinion, emerged around the year 2000. And photo-sharing sites, such as Flickr and Photobucket, became a part of the Internet landscape in the early 2000s.

The first service to combine all of these features into a single social network was Friendster, in 2003. Friendster also introduced the concepts of "friends" and "friending" to the social web; it all came from the name, not surprisingly.

Friendster, the original social network

Friendster is the fun and safe way to organize your social life

New to Friendster?
Join now - it's free and takes less than a minute to sign up.

Join Now

Already a member?

email
password

☐ remember my email

Log In

Forgot your password?
Problems logging in?

Find out why more than 13 million people have joined Friendster, the FREE online service to:
- Stay in touch with your friends
- Find and reconnect with old friends
- See how your friends are connected
- Be reminded about friends' birthdays
- Meet new people through your friends
- Have fun browsing people who share similar interests

Friendster enjoyed immediate popularity (more than 3 million users within the first few months of operations), but ran into technical problems associated with that growth and was soon surpassed by MySpace, which launched later the same year. MySpace became the Web's most popular social network in June 2006, and remained so for almost two years.

Friendster and MySpace were part of the first wave of social media. The second wave formed in 2004, when a site originally known as "thefacebook" came on the scene. What eventually became known as just "Facebook" was originally launched as a site where college students could socialize online, but quickly opened the door for users of all ages.

The Social Network

The story of Facebook's genesis was told in the 2010 film, *The Social Network*. While some elements of the film are clearly fictitious, it's actually a fairly accurate retelling of events.

This broadening in Facebook's user base led to a huge increase in both users and usage, with Facebook surpassing MySpace in April 2008. Today, Facebook is not only the number-one social network, it's also the number-two site on the entire Internet, with more than 1 billion users of all ages. That's a pretty big deal.

Facebook, today's largest social network

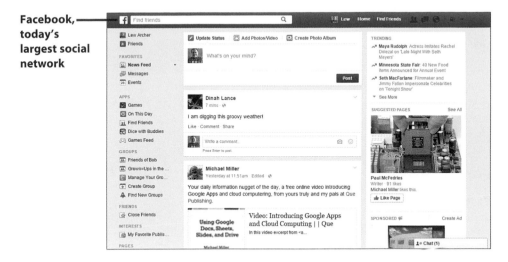

Facebook isn't the only social network today, however. Hot on its heels are several social media that are more specialized than the general-interest Facebook. These newer contenders include Twitter (specializing in short text-only messages), Pinterest (which lets users share images they find all across the Web), LinkedIn (targeting business professionals), and Instagram (which is all about photo sharing). None of these social media is near as big as Facebook, but they serve different needs.

Who Uses Social Media—and Why

With all that social media have to offer, it's not surprising that so many people use them day in and day out. As with many new technologies, social media started out being used almost exclusively by high school and college students. (That's how the Internet itself took off, after all.) But over time, social media spread from the young generation to the general public, including older users like you and me.

While different social media appeal to different groups of users, the audience for social media in general has evolved into something approximating that of the general population—which means that more and more older people are getting social. Taking Facebook as an example, 63% of those aged 50 to 64 use

Facebook, as do 56% of all Internet users aged 65 and older. (These statistics come from the Pew Internet and American Life Project, for the year 2014.)

Differing Popularity

Of course, not all social media are as popular with older users. Twitter, for example, is used by just 10% of Internet users aged 65 and older, and by 12% of those aged 50 to 64. (In contrast, 37% of those aged 18 to 29 use Twitter.)

In practice, then, social media such as Facebook appeal to all sorts of people and for all sorts of reasons, including:

- Friends and family members who want to keep in touch
- People looking for long-lost friends
- Business colleagues looking for collaboration and networking
- Singles who want to meet and match up with other singles
- Hobbyists looking for others who share their interests
- Classmates who need study partners and homework advice
- Musicians, actors, and celebrities (and politicians!) connecting with their fans

What all these types of users have in common is that they desire easy and immediate interaction with friends, family members, co-workers, and followers. With social media, it's easy to interact with other people via public posts, private communication, event calendars, and even community-based games and applications.

In short, the various social media available today help you keep in contact with large numbers of people without having to interact personally with each and every individual. It's effective and efficient communication.

>>>*Go Further*

DEMOGRAPHIC MIGRATION

I find it interesting that so many technologies are first adapted by younger users, but then eventually migrate upward and outward to older folks and the general population. That's how it happened not just with social media, but also with other Internet-based technologies.

Take email, for instance. Email first became a thing back in the early 1990s, when students on college campuses got used to sending private messages to their friends over their schools' private email systems. They didn't want to give up their email when they graduated, which led them to seek out primitive email systems out in the real world, including those connected to America Online and other commercial online services. This commercialization of email not only encouraged Hotmail and other companies to get into the email business, but also nudged many large and small businesses to adopt email for their own intraoffice communications. Before you knew it, it wasn't just the college kids using email anymore; everybody, regardless of age, had their own email address. It migrated upward from the kiddies to the adults.

It's been the same thing with social media. Friendster and MySpace had particular appeal to high school and college students, and Facebook was born on a college campus exclusively for the use of college students. It didn't take long, however, for these younger users to move out into the real world and take their love for (and reliance on) social media to a larger audience. Soon the twentysomethings became thirtysomethings, who communicated with fortysomethings, who dragged their fifty- and sixtysomething friends and relatives along for the ride. What started as a fun diversion for the younger generation became a useful means of sharing (and a fun diversion, too) for older generations.

So if you want to know what you and your friends will be using next, look to the high school and college kids. What they use today, we'll probably be using tomorrow.

Why You'll Want to Use Social Media

Where many younger users tend to sign in to a social network when they wake up in the morning and not sign out until they go to bed at night, older users tend not to be as obsessed with social media. We might check into Facebook or Pinterest a few times a day, but they don't monopolize our lives. Or at least they shouldn't.

Instead, those of us aged 50 and up tend to use social media on a more occasional basis to keep tabs on what friends, family members, and colleagues are up to. We are not typically as addicted to social media as our children and grandchildren are; we don't have to know what everyone is doing on a minute-by-minute basis. Instead, we can log in once or maybe twice a day and get the general drift of everyone's activities. That's enough information for most of us.

Grown-ups also use social media to reconnect with people we haven't seen in a while. A long while, sometimes. Personally, I use Facebook to hook up with old friends from high school and college, and to reconnect with former colleagues and those I might want to work with again. (I guarantee you'll find people on Facebook and other social media that you haven't thought about for a long time—which may not always be a good thing, I suppose…)

Finding old friends on Facebook

Search for Friends | Done |

Find friends from different parts of your life
Name
Search for someone

Mutual Friend
☐ Rudolfo Lasperi
☐ Bob Miller
☐ Jesse Stone
Enter another name

Hometown
☐ Carmel, Indiana
Enter another city

Current City
☐ Saint Paul, Minnesota
Enter another city

High School
☐ Ben Davis High School
Enter another high school

College or University
☐ Indiana University
Enter another college or unive…

Social media is also a great way for family members—especially extended families—to keep abreast of comings and goings. It might take a lot of effort to personally write your cousins and aunts and uncles and nieces and nephews and stepchildren and in-laws and all the rest, but a single Facebook status update will do the job of multiple letters and emails. You can also use social media to share family photos with the rest of your family, which is a ton easier than printing and mailing photos manually.

Speaking of family members, social media is also great for keeping in touch with what your children and grandchildren are up to, without them actually having to have a conversation with you about it. All you have to do is add your kids to your social media friends lists, and you'll see all the posts they make public. (That's unless they adjust their privacy settings to exclude you from their most private thoughts, which if they're smart, they'll do.)

Of course, there are plenty of ways for adult users to waste time on social media, just as our kids do. I know a fair number of supposed grown-ups who get addicted to Candy Crush Saga and other social games, and spend way too much time playing them. Useless social media activity isn't the sole province of the young; us oldsters can also spend hours doing essentially nothing useful online.

Bottom line, those of us 50 and up use social media for many of the same reasons that younger folks do, but in a smarter and less intrusive fashion. Or so we'd like to think, anyway.

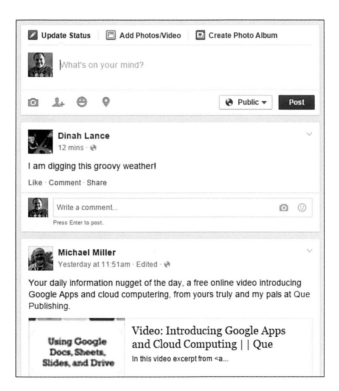

In this chapter, you discover the best ways to post on social media, and what you should and shouldn't post.

What to Share—and What *Not* to Share—on Social Media

Social media is all about being social, and sharing your thoughts, experiences, photos, and more. That said, is everything you do and think ripe for sharing? What do your online friends want to see—and what would they rather *not* see from you?

Deciding what to share on social media is a delicate dance. Share too much (or the wrong things) and your friends will quit reading your posts and maybe even "unfriend" you. Share too little and your friends will forget you're even there. You need to figure out just what kinds of things to share, and how often.

How to Write a Proper Post

When it comes to posting something on social media, *how* you post is often as important as *what* you post. There's a right way to post your messages, and many wrong ways to do so.

Messages, Posts, and Status Updates

Don't get confused by the nomenclature. What you call a message probably goes by a different name on different social networks. Some call messages *posts*, others call them *status updates*. On Twitter, the messages you post are called *tweets*. They're all just different names for the same thing—the thoughts and information you share with others online.

Keep It Short

A short post——I am digging this groovy weather!

Anything you post to Facebook or Twitter or most other social media should be concise and to the point. Even though most social media will accept posts as long as you like (Twitter being the exception here, with a 140-character limit), that doesn't mean that you *should* ramble on for multiple paragraphs. Most people don't really read the posts in their news feeds; instead, they graze through them, kind of like reading headlines in a newspaper.

News Feed

A *news feed* (on some networks simply called a *feed*) displays a stream of posts or status updates from your friends or contacts on that social network.

You see, a social media post is not a blog post or an entry in your diary; it's more like an item in a news ticker. Put another way, a social media post is a news bulletin, not a feature story. So say what you need to say and be done with it.

This means you should try to keep your posts to no more than a few sentences. Just long enough to get your point across, but not so long that readers will get bored. If your posts are too long, your friends will simply skip over them. Shorter is sweeter.

When you don't have the space to provide a lot of background information in a particular post, you can also link to more information. If there's more behind the story, include a link to a web page that offers more details. Readers can click the link to read more on the linked-to site.

Keep It Casual

Sentence fragment

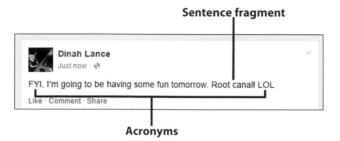

Acronyms

In your goal of creating short but memorable posts, know that you can take some grammatical shortcuts. Unlike formal letter or email writing, when posting to social media, you don't have to use full sentences or proper grammar. In fact, it's okay to use common abbreviations and acronyms, such as BTW (by the way) and LOL (laughing out loud).

To that end, your writing style should be casual, not formal. Write like you speak. Imagine yourself sitting with a group of friends in your local bar or coffeeshop, telling them the latest piece of information. Whatever you would say to them is what you should write in your post. Avoid unnecessary formality; casual is good.

That doesn't mean you can get sloppy. While you don't have to use complete, proper grammar and punctuation, you want to avoid unnecessary misspellings. Misspelled words mark you as less informed than you might actually be and cause people to take you less seriously. Take the time to spell things correctly.

A post in all caps—AVOID

Also, and this is important, while you don't have to use 100% totally correct grammar and punctuation, you should never write in all capital letters. WHEN YOU WRITE IN ALL CAPS, IT LOOKS LIKE YOU'RE YELLING. Learn how to use the Shift key and *not* the Caps Lock key on your keyboard. You don't have to properly capitalize every word (especially if you're typing on your smartphone), but don't capitalize every word and every letter. Just don't.

Show It If You Can

A post accompanied by a photograph

The world around us is becoming more visual. To that end, more and more social media posts include images, either as the sole post or to supplement the accompanying text message. Pictures are important.

Let's face it, when reading onscreen, your eyes are drawn to any pictures on the page. We like looking at pictures, especially pictures of people. If you have a picture in your post, more people will look at it than if the post were text-only. If you want to draw attention to a post, include a picture. It's that simple.

In fact, some social media are built around image sharing. Pinterest and Instagram, for example, are visual social networks. Yes, you can add descriptions to your Pinterest pins and Instagram photos, but it's the images that you're sharing.

You can include images with your posts to most other social media, too. Even Twitter, the king of text-based messages, now lets you include photos with your tweets. My Facebook News Feed is almost exclusively composed of status updates with photos. Like I said, we live in a visual world—and we need to communicate visually.

This may mean uploading a photo to accompany the text message you planned to post. It may mean posting only a photo, taken with your smartphone or previously stored on your computer. If social media help you document your life, an important part of that documentation will be in the form of digital photographs.

>>>*Go Further*

HOW OFTEN SHOULD YOU POST?

One of the most common questions I get concerns frequency. When it comes to sharing on social media, just how often should you post?

The general answer to this question is that you should post frequently—but not too frequently. Social media create communities, and to be a member of any such community, you have to actively participate. While you aren't required to post anything to social media, if you wait too long between posts, people will forget that you're there. You have to be somewhat active, or you might as well not be there at all.

Conversely, if you post too frequently, that might be perceived as overbearing or annoying. You can overpost and wear out your welcome. If you have too many pointless posts clogging your friends' feeds, they'll shut you down. Nobody likes a conversation hog, either online or in the real world. Don't bombard your friends with too much information.

As to specific recommendations, that differs from site to site. When it comes to Facebook, the best frequency is somewhere between once a week and a few times per day. Younger users tend to expect more frequent postings, but for us grown-ups, once every day or two is probably good.

If we're talking about Twitter, those users expect more frequent postings—several times a day. Pinterest users are comfortable with a few pins a day, often done in batches. And LinkedIn's business/professional focus argues for fewer postings, once or twice a week, tops.

Probably the best way to judge how often to post is to examine the posts in your own news feed. Look at those friends whose posts you look forward to, opposed to those you get tired of reading. The person who leaves you asking for more probably has the frequency right.

Posting Things That People Want to Read

When you use social media, it's easy to think that it's all about *you*. It's you writing your posts, after all, discussing things that happened to you and are of interest to you. It's your life you're sharing!

Except that it really isn't. Yes, you are posting things about you, but you want your friends to read those things and interact with you about them. If you're selfish about what you post, your friends will tune you out and you'll only be talking to yourself. As with any social situation, you want to initiate a conversation—and that means keeping your audience in mind when you post.

In other words, you need to post about things that are of interest to your friends. If a post is only of interest to you, no one else will read it.

News Updates

One very important use of social media is to keep your family and friends up-to-date on your latest personal news. One post can inform a large number of people about something important; it's a lot more efficient than sending out dozens of emails or making tons of phone calls.

Important information in a post

Dinah Lance
Just now · 🌐

Gloria graduates from college tomorrow. We're so proud of her!

Like · Comment · Share

What, then, counts as interesting information that your friends will want to read? Here are some suggestions:

- Post things that are important to you and your friends. We're talking moments and events that are important to *you*, but that you also think your *friends* might care about, too.

- Post things that your friends and family want to know about. Friends typically want to know if you've done or seen something interesting, taken a vacation, met a mutual friend, and such. If you think someone's interested in it, post it.

- Post about major life events—things in your life that your friends and family *need* to know about. These are important moments and events, such as anniversaries, birthdays, graduations, celebrations, and the like.

- Post important news updates. If you have recently been ill or hospitalized, update your friends on how you're doing. If you have a new job or a new volunteer position, let your friends know. If you've moved to a new house or condo, spread the word via a social media post. If something important has happened in your life, update friends and family via social media.

- Post important news about your spouse or partner. Your social media updates don't always have to be about you. Many of your friends are likely mutual friends of your spouse, so if anything major has happened to your partner, include that information in your status update—especially if she can't post herself, for whatever reason.

- Post important news about other family members. You might know something about a cousin or nephew that others in your family might not have yet heard. Share your information with other family members via a social media post.

- Post about mutual friends. It's tough to keep track of all your old friends. Start the chain going by posting what you know, and let your other friends pass it on to their friends, too.

- Post about upcoming events. If there's something coming up that's important to you and interesting to your friends, let them know. Maybe you're singing at an upcoming concert or church service, maybe you have a big golf tournament, maybe you're hosting or participating in a big charity event. If you want your friends to know about (and maybe attend) the event, then post about it.

- Post interesting thoughts. Look, you've come this far in life; you've earned your opinions. Share your wisdom with your friends and family via Facebook status updates—in a non-controversial, inoffensive way, if you can.

It's Not All Good

Is It Really Interesting?

Just because something is interesting to you doesn't mean it's interesting to anyone else. The fact that you went to a concert or read a good book is interesting; that you woke up with a headache or just had a cup of tea is not. I've seen too many posts of things my friends find "cute" (cats, in particular) that I could not care less about. Try to look at things from someone else's perspective before you post.

Things You Probably *Shouldn't* Share Online

With all the interesting bits of information you can and should share via social media, there are also lots of things you probably shouldn't.

Social networks are meant to be social; they want your posts to be seen by as many people as possible. This isn't private email we're talking about. Social networks are *public* networks, not private ones.

Because everything is so public, you can do a lot of damage to yourself by posting something stupid. And people post stupid, harmful stuff all the time. It's like some folks forget that social media are public media, not private media. Just remember, everything you post can and probably will become public—and ultimately come back to haunt you.

What and how much personal information to share via Facebook and other social media depends to a degree on your personal comfort level and your personal life. But in general, you shouldn't share any information that might prove embarrassing to you or your family, or that might compromise your current job or associations, or future job prospects. (Or, for that matter, that might make you vulnerable to identity theft.)

Naturally, what all this means is going to differ from person to person. If you serve on a homeowner's association filled with ultra-conservative neighbors, for example, you might not want them to know that you're a dyed-in-the-wool liberal. And if all your golfing buddies are agnostics, you might not want to publicize that you're a born-again Christian.

But it goes further than that. If you're preaching the "just say no" drug message to your children or grandchildren, you might not want to list *Cheech & Chong's Up in Smoke* as one of your favorite movies; it might compromise your integrity on the matter just a bit. For that matter, you might want to hide all those photos that show you drinking margaritas on the beach, for both your kids' sake and to ward off any awkward questions from teetotalling employers or neighbors.

In fact, pictures can be more damaging than words. A picture of you holding a cigarette in your hand could be used by your insurance company to raise your health insurance rates. Photos of you partying hardy or just acting goofy can raise doubts about your decision-making abilities. Do you really want your pastor or your grandkids or your ex-husband's lawyer to see you in compromising positions?

The same goes with the content you post on social media sites. There are stories, some of them true, of careless (and carefree) employees posting about this afternoon's golf game when they were supposed to be home sick from work. Employers (and spouses and just about anyone else) can and will keep track of you online, if you're stupid enough to post all your comings and goings.

And it's not just factual stuff. Spouting off your opinions is a common-enough online activity, but some people will disagree with you or take more serious offense. Do you really want to get into an online argument over something you posted in haste after a few drinks at the club?

For that matter, it's a really bad idea to use social media to criticize the people you work for, the people you work with, or the people you associate with in the community. Posting about how much you hate the president of the neighborhood association will eventually get back to her, and then you have a whole bunch of fences to mend.

The Golden Rule

When posting to social media, follow the online golden rule: Post only about others as you would have them post about you. If you can't say something nice, don't say anything at all.

With some social media, such as Facebook, you have the option of making a given post visible only to those on your friends list. While it might be tempting to share intimate details with your online friends, think about who these "friends" really are. How many of your social media friends are close, intimate friends? How many are merely acquaintances, or just people you work with or went to school with? How many are people you really don't know at all?

If you have a hundred or so people on your friends list, that's a hundred or so people who could be reading about how you hate your kids, or how you cheated the IRS, or how you really feel about the people you work with. It's not hard to imagine how this personal information can come back to haunt you.

What you have to remember is that on social media, you're not invisible. It's a public community; everything you post may be readable by anyone. Post only that information that would be safe enough for your family, friends, and co-workers to read.

You see, on social media, discretion is definitely the better part of valor. When in doubt, don't post it. It's okay to keep some thoughts to yourself; you don't have to post every little thing you think or that happens to you.

It's Not All Good

How Do Others Do It?

If you're not sure whether or how to post something on social media, you don't have to reinvent any wheels. Chances are someone else has faced the same dilemma and discovered the right (or wrong) way to deal with this situation.

To this end, one of the best ways to learn proper social media etiquette is to observe how others do it. Observe how and what your friends post (especially those you find particularly engaging), and mimic their behavior. If it works for them, it'll probably work for you, too. As I said, there's no reason to reinvent the wheel; learn from the people who came before you.

Ten Things to Avoid When Posting Online

With the previous advice in mind, here are ten things you probably shouldn't do when posting to social media.

1. Don't Post if You Don't Have Anything to Say

Some of the most annoying people on Facebook, Twitter, and other social media are those that post their every action and movement. ("I just woke up." "I'm reading my mail." "I'm thinking about having lunch." "That coffee was delicious.") Post if there's something interesting happening, but avoid posting just to be posting. Think about what you like to read about other people, and post in a similar fashion.

2. Don't Pick a Fight

Many people use social media as a platform for their opinions. While it may be okay to share your opinions with close (that is, real-world) friends, spouting off in a public forum is not only bad form, it's a way to incite a *flame war*—an unnecessary online war of words.

So don't deliberately post controversial opinions just to stir the pot—and don't feel compelled to add your (conflicting) opinions as comments on other posts. Social media are not the places to argue politics, religion, or other sensitive subjects. Save your inflammatory comments for your family's Thanksgiving dinner.

3. Don't Post Anything That Could Be Used Against You

Want to put your job in jeopardy? Then by all means, you should post negative comments about your workplace or employer. Want your partner to walk out on you? Then share your petty personal beefs with the entire online world. You get the picture; anything you post online can and probably will be used against you. So don't post negative personal comments or attacks that are better kept private. If you're in doubt, don't post it; it's better to be safe than sorry.

4. Don't Post Overly Personal Information

Along the same lines, think twice before sharing the intimate details of your private life—including embarrassing photographs. Discretion is a value us older folks should maintain; there's no reason for posting pictures of you falling down drunk at the holiday office party, or baring it all on the beach during your last vacation. Leave some of the details to imagination.

Similarly, not everyone wants to hear the gory details of your latest knee surgery, what you found in your teenaged son's room yesterday, or what color underwear you're wearing—or if you're not wearing underwear at all. There's the concept of TMI (too much information), and you want to avoid including TMI in your social media posts. If you'd rather not see those kinds of details about other people, don't subject them to your similar details, either. There's such a thing as oversharing.

5. Don't Gripe

Building on that last tip, the last thing I (and lots of others) want to find in our news feeds are your private gripes. We really, really don't care if your husband leaves the toilet seat up or if your next-door neighbor hasn't mowed his lawn in two weeks. Oh, it's okay to grouse and be grumpy from time to time, but don't use social media as your personal forum for petty grievances. If you have a personal problem, deal with it. You don't have to share *everything*, you know. Whining gets old really fast.

This is especially the case when you're complaining about the people you work with or deal with on a daily basis. Yeah, I know, your boss (or the leader of the neighborhood commission) is a jerk, but it's nothing I can do anything about. On the other hand, if this jerk sees your posts, you've just created a bit of an awkward situation for yourself. Remember, social media are public media, and if you post it, your boss or group leader or whomever will eventually see it (especially if troublemaking co-workers point it out to him). Don't post anything that you don't want someone to see. Period.

6. Don't Post Personal Contact Information

As nice as Facebook and other social media are for renewing old acquaintances, they can also put you in contact with people you really don't want to be in contact with. So don't make it easy for disreputable people or unwanted old boyfriends to find you offline; avoid posting your phone number, email address, and home address.

Posting this sort of information can also put you at risk for identity theft. Avoid posting anything that a digital thief could use to gain access to your personal accounts. That means not only your address, phone number, and such, but also information that could be used to guess your passwords—your mother's maiden name, your birthdate, your pet's name, your favorite color, and so forth. And definitely never, ever post your Social Security number.

A large part of keeping yourself safe online is simply not doing anything dumb. Posting personal information on social media is dumb. So don't do it.

7. Don't Post Your Constant Whereabouts

For that matter, you don't need to broadcast your every movement; thieves don't need to know when you're away from home. When you post that you're having a wonderful dinner downtown, or enjoying your week-long vacation in Florida, you're advertising to anyone and everyone that your house is empty and ripe for the picking. You don't need to give the bad guys such a blatant heads up.

Similarly, you don't want people you don't like to know where you're at right now. If someone is out to get you, they don't need to know that you're enjoying cocktails at the corner of Fifth and Main. You want to minimize contact with unfriendly people, not make it easier for them to harass you.

In short, it's okay to post where you were *after the fact*, but not beforehand. You want to keep your current whereabouts private.

Similarly, don't post information about your daily or weekly routines. You don't want to tell the bad guys that you're always in yoga class on Wednesdays at 4:00, or have a standing golf game every Saturday morning at the club. Keep your routines private.

8. Don't Post Rumors, Hoaxes, and Urban Legends

Social media is rife with rumors, half-truths, and misinformation. Did you hear the one about the sick child who's collecting get well cards, or needs you to "like" or share his post? Or the one about the government secretly plotting martial law? Or the "advice" that entering your PIN in reverse at an ATM will summon the police? Or that Macaulay Caulkin (or Bill Nye or Will Smith or some other well-known celebrity) has died—in spite of his protests to the contrary?

These posts are all false. They spread lies and untruths, and take up valuable bandwidth in your news feed. Some people obviously believe them; others see them for what they are—urban legends and conspiracy theories that mislead the gullible among us.

Unfortunately, these questionable posts are often quite popular, going viral as they're shared from one person to another. In the old days, your crazy relatives shared them via email; today, they're shared via Facebook and Twitter instead. If you've been on social media at all, you've no doubt seen your share of them.

These posts are easily identified as what they are, which is total cow manure. You should never, ever share or retweet these sorts of posts. You should never start new ones yourself, unless it's very clearly a joke. A lot of people believe these things, and we don't need to contribute to their lack of intelligence. Just ignore them.

9. Don't Post Pictures of People Without Their Permission

Social media is great for sharing things that you do. But you shouldn't use social media to post too much about other people, without their permission. It's okay to let your friends know what other mutual friends are up to, but you can't speak for those other people. Posting information that's publicly known is one thing, but sharing personal secrets is quite another.

Similarly, you shouldn't post pictures of other people without first getting their permission—especially if those pictures are in any way compromising. Even though *you* may be okay with it, a lot of people don't want their mugs plastered all over Facebook or Instagram. Some people wish to remain more private, and we need to respect their wishes.

Now, this can be a tricky issue. What if you're taking pictures at a neighborhood block party—are those pictures of your neighbors okay to post? What about pictures you took at your son's graduation or your granddaughter's birthday party? These are all public events, and thus might be fair game—until you run into that one neighbor or parent who doesn't want her or her children's pictures posted publicly. Like I said, it's tricky.

The best approach is to ask permission before you post. Most people will say okay. If you can't ask permission, the safe thing to do is to not post that particular photo of that particular person. Or you can go ahead and post it but take it down if someone complains. I have to recommend the more discreet approach, but I do admit to posting without permission on occasion.

Some venues will ask that you don't post pictures of their events. In this instance, respect the request. I recently attended my grandson's preschool graduation ceremony, and the teachers explicitly asked that group pictures not be posted to Facebook or other social media, because some parents don't want their children thus exposed. That was a fair request, and one I honored. You should do the same in similar situations.

Finally, consider which pictures of your kids and grandkids are appropriate to post. That picture of your granddaughter in her swim suit may be cute to you, but lascivious to someone else—and potentially embarrassing to her. We all want to show off our kids and grandkids, and I'm the worst offender in this, but sometimes family pictures should be limited to family only.

10. Don't Post Sensitive Information

Finally, if your work or social activities involve sensitive or confidential information, for goodness sakes, don't spill that information online. Avoid posting about the project you're working on, even that you're working on a project. Do not share details that competitors or opponents might find useful. Do not violate any confidentiality agreements, and do not abuse your employer's trust. Social media is great for sharing what you do on your personal time, but not at all proper for sharing what you do during work hours. Leave it at work; don't share it on Facebook.

Joining a Conversation—or Not

Given the social nature of social media, you're encouraged to comment on other people's posts, to join in the conversation, and to share what you read with others. But should you always jump in the middle of an online conversation? And are there posts you see that you shouldn't share?

When to Join a Conversation, and When to Bow Out

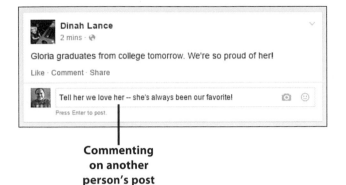

Commenting on another person's post

Social networks and online message boards let you comment on the posts that others make, and in the process, create ongoing conversations. You comment on a post, someone comments on your comment, you respond to that, and on it goes. It's part of what makes social media so social.

Most social media conversations are good. Some aren't. Some devolve into online shouting matches. Others just get silly. Still others would be better served as a private chat between two people, not as a public message thread.

When, then, should you join the conversation? And when should you exercise more restraint and not add your two cents' worth?

Here are some do's and don'ts for joining conversations in social media:

- **Do** join a conversation when input is asked for or encouraged.

- **Don't** join a conversation if your input is no more substantive than "Me too" or "You bet."

- **Do** join a conversation if you have knowledge or experience that would be useful or interesting.

- **Don't** join a conversation if you have absolutely nothing new or unique to add—or if you simply don't know what you're talking about.

- **Do** join a conversation to lend support to a friend. Sometimes a comment can be like a virtual hug or pat on the back, and that's a good thing.

- **Don't** join a conversation just to cause trouble. We're talking randomly negative comments that have little bearing on the original post, save to raise the hackles of those reading. This is commonly called *trolling*, and you shouldn't do it. If it's obvious that you're among a group of right-wing Republicans, there's not a whole lot of good that can come out of posting your left-wing Democratic opinions; you're not going to convert anybody—you're just going to make them mad at you. As tempting as it might be to sound off against those you disagree with, there's really no point in being a troublemaker.

- **Do** join a conversation if you can move it forward, by providing additional information or viewpoints.

- **Don't** join a conversation just to hijack it in a different direction. It's not your conversation, it's the person's who started it. Keep things on track!

In short, an online conversation is just like one in the real world. If you can add something to the mix without derailing it, then join in. If you have nothing important to add, then don't.

What to Share—and What *Not* to Share

Sharing another person's post

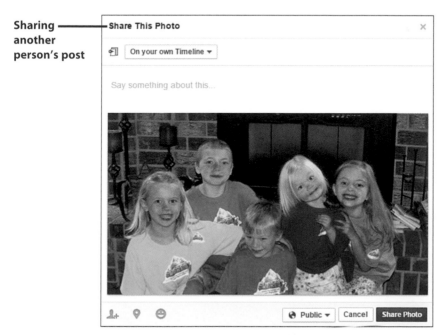

Sometimes you run into a post from someone that you think your friends might find interesting. Maybe it's a link to an informative web page. Maybe it's a cute photograph. Maybe it's just some interesting information. Facebook and other social media let you share these posts with your online friends. (Twitter calls this *retweeting*.)

The problem is, if you share too many things on your news feed, people are going to start tuning out. You want them to see the interesting things you share, which is difficult if you're clogging the feed with too many uninteresting or irrelevant things you've shared.

The key, as with all posting, is to know what your friends will find interesting and what they'll find frivolous. Here are some tips:

- **Do** share items of direct interest to your online friends.

- **Don't** share items that you find interesting but your friends won't.

- **Do** share items your friends are likely not to have seen otherwise.

- **Don't** share items that you've seen repeatedly online. Chances are that your friends have already seen it, too.

- **Do** share funny pictures and videos. If they made you laugh, they'll probably amuse your friends, too.

- **Don't** share items that you haven't independently verified. The last thing you want to do is spread inaccurate information or urban legends—or even web URLs that lead nowhere.

- **Do** share posts from friends and family members, if they're relevant.

- **Don't** share photos of people who don't want their pictures shared. For that matter, don't share any private information that you have in your possession.

- **Do** share pictures of your younger children and grandchildren. People like looking at cute family pictures—as long as you don't overdo it. (And as long as the pictures aren't inappropriate, of course.)

- **Don't** share inflammatory messages, photos, and hate speech. If you can't be civil and respect others' opinions and rights, you don't belong on social media.

When to Tag Yourself—and Others—in Photos

Lew Archer (Me)

Michael Michards

Michael Miller

Bob Miller

Rudolfo Lasperi

Tom French — **Tagging another person in a photo**

Dinah Lance

Jesse Stone

Type any name

Click on the photo to start tagging. **Done Tagging**

Then there's the issue of *tagging*, identifying yourself or someone else in a picture that's been posted online. Facebook and other social media let you tag people in photos; in fact, many people tag themselves and their friends when they post their pictures. You can also jump in after the fact and tag people you know (yourself included) when viewing others' photos.

At first blush, identifying people in a picture sounds like a good thing, like you're helping out the person who posted that photo and didn't add any tags. Maybe you know someone in the photo he didn't, after all.

The problem is that not everyone wants to be singled out online. Tagging a person has the unfortunate effect of making that photo visible to all of that person's friends, even if she doesn't want her friends to see it. Maybe the photo is less than flattering, or records embarrassing or unwise behavior, or places that person in a place where he doesn't want people to see him. In essence, tagging a person without his knowledge or permission can cause all sorts of problems for the person being tagged, even if it's just giving that person a little more visibility than he might want.

The bottom line on this one is pretty clear. Unless you know the person wants to be tagged, you shouldn't tag him. Maybe that means asking first, maybe it means not tagging that person in the photo, maybe it means not posting the photo at all. Some people like to remain as anonymous as possible; you should respect that decision and err on the side of caution.

Using Social Media—Safely and Privately

How safe is social media? If you use social media, is your personal information at risk? Can you be harmed using social media?

The reality is that social media is as safe, or as risky, as anything on the Internet. If you use social media intelligently and responsibly, you can minimize whatever risks exist.

Is It Safe to Use Social Media?

There are potential hazards involved in virtually every online activity, from reading emails to web browsing. Such hazards also exist with the use of social media, such as Facebook.

What kinds of hazards are we talking about? There are both major and minor ones, including the following:

- **Computer viruses and other malware.** Like any website, posts on a social networking site can contain links to computer viruses, spyware, and other forms of malware. If you click on a bad link, often disguised as a link to an interesting website or application, you can infect your computer with this type of malicious software.

Malware

A *computer virus* is a malicious software program that can cause damage to an infected computer. *Spyware* is a similar but different software program that obtains information from your computer without your knowledge or consent. Both viruses and spyware are forms of malicious software—*malware* for short.

- **Spam.** Users who publicly post their email addresses on Facebook and other social media can find themselves the target of unwanted junk email, or spam. Spammers harvest email addresses from social networking sites and add these addresses to their email mailing lists for sending spam messages.

- **Identity theft.** Posting personal information publicly on Facebook and similar social media can result in *identity theft*. Identity thieves use this public information to assume a user's identity on the social network or on other websites; to apply for credit cards and loans in the user's name; to legitimize undocumented foreign workers; and to gain access to the user's banking and credit card accounts.

Identity Theft

Identity theft is a form of fraud in which one person pretends to be someone else, typically by stealing personal information, such as a bank number, credit card number, or Social Security number. The intent of identity theft is often to steal money or obtain other benefits.

- **Cyberbullying.** It's unfortunate, but many people employ social media to bully people they dislike. This is particularly common among school-age users, but can happen to people of any age. Some online bullies post threatening messages on their victims' profile pages; other go to the extreme of creating fake profile pages for their victims, full of embarrassing fictitious information. Cyberbullying is particularly troublesome, as it can be completely anonymous but have the same debilitating effects as physical bullying.

- **Online stalking.** Online stalkers like to follow their victims from one website to another. If granted friend status, these online bullies—often pretending to be someone that they're not—will try to become close to you, whether for their own personal enjoyment or to cause you discomfort, embarrassment, or actual harm.

- **Physical stalking or harassment.** Some online predators take their stalking into the physical world. This is facilitated when you post personal information—including phone numbers and home addresses—on Facebook and other social networking sites. This information helps predators physically contact their victims, which can result in harassment or even physical violence.

- **Robbery.** Have you ever posted on Facebook about going out for dinner on a given evening, or about getting ready to take a long vacation? When you do so, you're telling potential robbers when your home will be empty—and that your belongings are ripe for the taking.

Scary stuff, all of it.

That said, social media is only as hazardous—or as safe—as you make it. If you post a plethora of personal information, you'll be less safe than if you are more discreet. If you avoid posting personal details about your life, you'll be safer from potential attackers or identity thieves than if you post liberally about your activities.

How do you avoid these potential dangers? Well, the only sure way to be completely safe is to delete all your profiles and cease using Facebook and other social media. Short of that, however, you can network in relative safety by being smart about what you post and what you respond to on the site.

Smarter Social Networking

I can provide you lots of advice on how to keep safe on social media. (And I will, I promise!) But all the tips I can supply boil down to this: You have to use your head. Safe social networking is smart social networking. While various social media have various privacy and security tools you can employ, nothing will keep you safer than thinking before you click. The riskiest behavior comes from not considering all the consequences of what you might do. The safest users are those that don't do dumb things. So don't do dumb things.

Repeat: Don't do dumb things.

Now, to the more detailed recommendations—all of which involve smarter social networking.

Think Before You Click

You'll see lots of posts in your news feeds with clickable links—to other websites, to online articles, to photos and videos on other sites, you name it. Not every link is what it seems to be, however.

Just as with email, many disreputable types like to "phish" for information by posting links that look to be one thing but are actually something quite different. A link might purport to take you to an interesting news story, but in fact drop you on a page full of annoying advertisements. Or it might look like an official Facebook or Twitter link, but instead lead to a phony (but official-looking) web page that tries to get you to enter your user name and password, while tricking you into revealing your personal information.

The reality is, there are a lot of links in social media that are something less than what they seem. Most of these deceptive links merely lead to advertising-laden pages (so-called *click farms*, because the owner gets paid whenever someone clicks on an ad). But others are more dangerous in the way they phish for personal information.

So take care before you click on any link you find in your social network news feed. That's true even if the link is in a post from a trusted friend; even trusted friends can be deceived. And after you click, be ready to hit the "back" button if what you see isn't what you expect.

Think Before You Post

Just as you need to be smart about what you click in friends' posts, you also need to be smart about what you post. As discussed in Chapter 2, "What to Share—and What *Not* to Share—on Social Media," the more personal information you share, the more you put yourself at risk for identity theft, online harassing, and real-world burglary and assault. Do not post, however innocently or inadvertently, your street address, phone number, email address, Social Security number, or the like.

For that matter, don't post anything that bad guys could use to guess your password to this or other accounts. That means don't post your pet's name, your mother's maiden name, your favorite high school teacher, your favorite color, and the like. Don't make it quite so easy for would-be hackers.

Don't Accept Every Friend Request

Social media encourage social interaction, so when you first sign up for a social network, you'll likely be bombarded by friend requests from people you barely remember. You don't have to say "yes" to all these requests; just because someone wants to be your friend doesn't mean you have to let them. Be choosy.

There's another reason not to blindly accept every friend request you receive. Some identify thieves like to create fake profiles in the hopes that people (like you!) will absently-mindedly accept them. Once in your friends list, these scammers have access to everything you post—which, if you aren't that smart about posting, can include private information the scammer can use to gain access to this or other online accounts.

And even if they're not crooks and thieves, don't assume that your online friends are your real friends. I have Facebook "friends" who I barely remember from high school. There are things I'd share with my real friends that I'd never in my life imagine sharing with these Facebook friends-in-name-only. Remember, a real friend is one you can email or call on the phone, not someone who may (or may not) read the stuff you post on Facebook.

Unfriend People Who Aren't Friendly

Just because you add someone to a social media friends list doesn't mean that person has to stay in your list. If you find someone is posting offensive messages, hijacking the comments on your messages, or just annoying you with too many cat pictures, you can "unfriend" that person. (*Unfriending* is the act of removing someone from a friends list.) In fact, it makes sense to cull your friends lists from time to time, to separate the wheat from the chaff. You want your news feeds to include interesting posts from people you care about, not be full of junk that doesn't matter to you.

Keep Your Contacts Private

Many social networking sites seek to help you add people to your friends list, by volunteering to sift through your email or phone contacts lists for people who are also on that social network. If you let a social network scan your address book or contacts list, the site might use this information to send advertisements (or advertisements disguised as "your friend likes" messages) to these friends. Not only are these fake endorsement messages annoying, they may be sent to people who are in your lists but who you don't actually communicate with on a daily basis.

It's best to keep your lists separate. Don't give social networks access to your phone or email contacts. It's not good policy.

Don't Download Third-Party Applications

Some social media, such as Facebook, enable third parties to install applications that extend the functionality of their sites. The problem is that many of these third-party apps gain access to and use your personal information (including the names in your friends list) in ways you may not approve of. Some rogue apps may even steal your personal information, including user names and passwords.

If you want to minimize your risk, don't install third-party apps for your social networks. If you do find an app you like, read the reviews and ask around to make sure the app is legitimate—and not overly intrusive.

Don't Play Social Games

Along the same lines, some of the social games available on Facebook and other sites can be extremely intrusive in how they access and use your personal information and friends lists. You really don't want the latest game you played to post your score (or requests for extras or support) to all your friends' news feeds, do you? While social games can be fun to play, they can also be the most annoying things you do online.

The ultimate solution is to not install or play any social games, period. (Good luck with that…) Short of this Draconian measure, you should examine the private policies and settings for any social game you want to play, and configure the settings in the least obtrusive way possible—or, if you have no other choice, avoid the game completely. It isn't worth sacrificing your (and your friends') privacy for a little gaming fun.

Social Games

Learn more about social games in Chapter 16, "Playing Social Games."

Configure Your Privacy and Security Settings

Speaking of privacy settings, most social media allow you to configure your personal privacy and security settings. This enables you to determine who sees what you post, and how the site uses your personal information. You need to learn about and configure the privacy and security settings for the social networks you use.

Facebook Privacy

Facebook is the Internet's largest social network. Learn more about Facebook's privacy and security settings in Chapter 8, "Configuring Facebook's Privacy Settings."

Use Strong Passwords

When you create an account with a given social network, you create a username (sometimes your email address) and password. As with all online accounts, you want to make your password as secure as possible, to make it more difficult for bad guys to gain access to your account. Follow these tips to create more secure passwords:

- Longer passwords are more secure. An 8-character password is more secure than a 6-character one.

- Combine capital and lowercase letters.

- Use a combination of letters, numbers, and special characters.

- Don't use easily guessable words, such as your last name, pet's name, your birthdate, and such.

- The best passwords appear to be totally random combinations of characters. (These are also the hardest passwords to remember, but still…)

Use Different Passwords for Each Account

If you have a Facebook account, Twitter account, and Pinterest account, create different passwords for each of them. If you use the same password for all accounts, anybody breaking into one of your accounts can gain access to all of them. (Similarly, don't use your Facebook account to log into other social media accounts; keep each account separate!)

Install Anti-Malware Tools on Your PC

Since computer viruses and spyware can be spread via social media, it's a good idea to install anti-malware tools on your computer. And, while anti-malware protection is a good back stop, you also want to avoid clicking on links in posts that may surreptitiously install malware on your system.

Trust Your Instincts

If you stumble across something suspicious in your news feed, trust your instincts and don't click that link or enter additional information. Don't get suckered into scams that request money or information or anything else. Social media are no more or less dangerous than the other social interactions you have in the outside world; there are bad guys out there, but you can avoid them by using your head. As I said earlier—don't be dumb!

Keeping Your Private Information Private

As you've learned, many of the potential hazards of social media revolve around personal information posted publicly. Since most social networks encourage you to enter some degree of private information about yourself (to facilitate more social interactions), it's possible that some or all of this information won't remain private.

Of first concern is the contact information you're required or just encouraged to enter, as well as any personal information you have in your profile for a given site. This can include your email address, street address, phone number, and so forth.

Fortunately, most social networks give you the option of hiding most of this information. Facebook, in particular, includes privacy settings that let you determine who can see what information—everyone (public), people on your friends list, or just yourself. You should use the site's privacy tools, discussed in Chapter 8, to hide as much personal information as possible from as many people as possible. And, of course, if such information is optional, you don't have to provide it in the first place.

The other private information that may become public is anything you might post as part of your regular status updates—what you did last night, who you're hanging out with, what you think of your family members or colleagues. These posts are typically public by default, which means that anyone can read them. As with your contact and profile information, however, you can employ the site's post-specific privacy settings to limit who can see the information in any given post. In this fashion, you can avoid full public disclosure of your private life if you so desire.

Again, be smart about how you configure your privacy settings and about what you post. The tools are yours to use—it's your responsibility to use them smartly.

>>>Go Further

HOW FACEBOOK USES YOUR PERSONAL INFORMATION

When we talk about social media security and privacy, it's good to look at Facebook, the Internet's largest social network. What Facebook does, others often mimic.

Unfortunately, the news isn't all good. That's because the personal information you provide to Facebook can be used by Facebook in a number of different ways—not all of which are to your benefit.

For example, Facebook can use your profile information—age, gender, education, and so forth—to display targeted third-party advertisements on your home page. Facebook may also track the other websites you visit and serve you ads based on the contents of those sites. These targeted ads may be marginally more appealing than generic advertisements, but are still, at least to some, a violation of your privacy; Facebook uses your own likes and dislikes for the company's benefit, to sell advertising.

Similarly, your profile information can be used for targeted invitations of various sorts. For example, Facebook may determine your interests from your profile data and invite you to play a particular game, use a certain application, join a given group, or add someone as a friend. These may appear to be helpful invitations, but still rely on the use of your private information.

It's also possible that Facebook may sell your personal information to interested third parties. Once Facebook sells the data to a particular company, you will typically receive one or more email messages advertising that company's wares. This isn't spam; you no doubt implicitly agreed that Facebook could share this data when you okayed the site's terms of service, and these are legitimate marketers. But it's still an annoying use or abuse of your private information.

And here's the rub: All of these uses of your private information are perfectly legal, and you probably agreed to them—assuming you read the fine print when you signed up for your account, of course. This points out the necessity of reading Facebook's terms of service before you sign up—and not participating if you don't like what you read.

Beyond these legal invasions of your privacy, there are many ways your personal information can be used illegally. These illegal invasions of your privacy can result in everything from spam to identity theft; you can guard against them by limiting the amount of personal information you publicly post on the social network site.

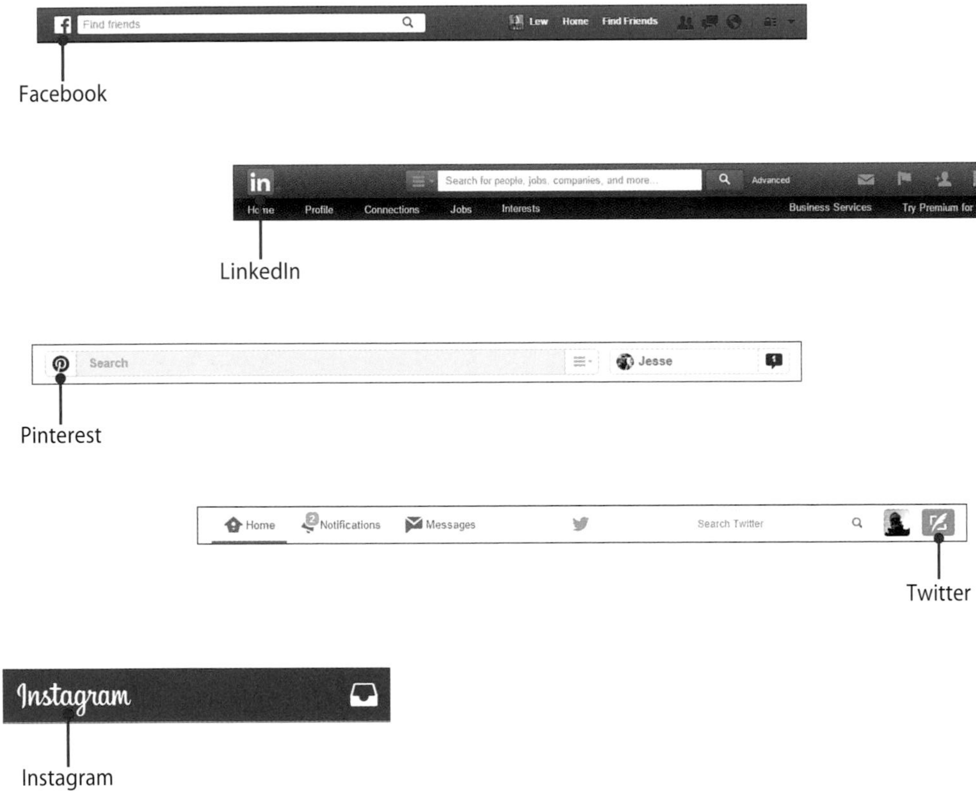

Find friends
Lew
Home
Find Friends
Facebook
Search for people, jobs, companies, and more...
Advanced
Home
Profile
Connections
Jobs
Interests
Business Services
Try Premium for free
LinkedIn
Search
Jesse
Pinterest
Home
Notifications
Messages
Search Twitter
Twitter
Instagram
Instagram

→ Examining Different Types of Social Media
→ Discovering the Top Social Media for Older Users

4

Comparing the Most Popular Social Media

I've talked a lot about Facebook, Pinterest, and Twitter, but there are
a lot more social media than just these, and they all service slightly
different purposes and user bases.

Examining Different Types of Social Media

Social media are those websites, services, and platforms that people
use to share experiences and opinions with one another. They cover
everything from social networks, where users share the details of their
own lives, to social bookmarking services, where users share sites and
articles they like.

Social Networks

The first type of social media is the *social network*. Social networks are unquestionably the most popular type of social media in use today.

The Google+ social network

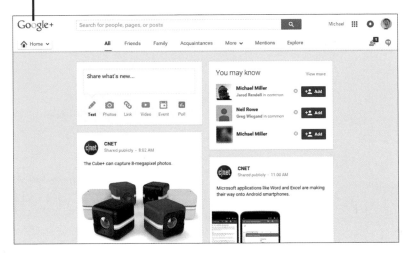

A social network is a large website or service that hosts a community of users and facilitates public and private communication between those users. Social networks enable users to share experiences and opinions with each other via short posts or status updates.

Some social networks, such as school or alumni networks, are devoted to a specific topic or community. Other social networks, such as Facebook, are more broad-based, which allows for communities within the overall network to be devoted to specific topics.

Because of their multi-faceted offerings, social networks appeal to a broad base of users. Young and old people alike use social networks, as do people of all genders, races, and income and education levels. Social networks help all these people keep up to date on what their friends are doing and keep them updated on what they are doing. They also help establish a sense of community based on shared experiences at school, in the workplace, or at play.

Most social networks revolve around users' posts or status updates. Users keep their friends informed of current activities via these short text or picture posts, then read updates from them via some sort of news feed. Everybody keeps up to date with what everybody else is doing.

Many social networks also offer other means of user-to-user communication, including private email and one-to-one instant messaging. Most social networks also include various forms of media sharing, including digital photographs, videos, and the like.

The most popular social networks today include:

- Facebook (www.facebook.com)
- LinkedIn (www.linkedin.com)
- Google+ (plus.google.com)

Google+

Google+ is a social network created by Google. While it's somewhat popular among younger, more tech-oriented users, it is not widely used by older users. You are more likely to find family members and friends on Facebook and LinkedIn.

Media Sharing Networks

A *media sharing network* like Pinterest and Instagram is a social network that focuses on images instead of text messages. There is less one-to-one communication, and more general photo and video sharing. It's like Facebook without all those bothersome words and sentences.

In a media sharing network, users post their own photos and videos, or links to images on various web pages. Their friends and followers then view, comment on, and share those posts with other people. The most popular images go viral, and are shared by thousands of interested users.

Because we've evolved into a very visual society, media sharing networks are becoming increasingly popular, particularly among users of mobile devices. It's easy to snap a picture with your smartphone and then post it to your network of choice. (For that matter, photo sharing on general social networks, such as Facebook, has become a very big part of the overall social experience.)

The Flickr media sharing network

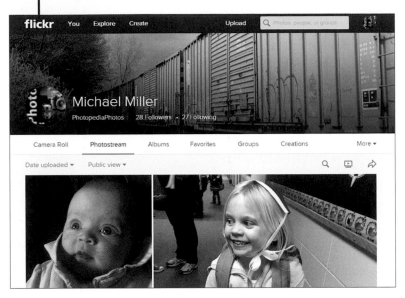

The most popular media sharing social networks today include:

- Pinterest (www.pinterest.com)
- Instagram (www.instagram.com)
- Flickr (www.flickr.com)

Microblogging Services

When you separate the short text messages or status updates from a social network into a separate feed, you have a *microblogging service*. Some microblogs, such as Twitter, exist primarily to distribute short text posts from individual users to groups of followers; other microblogs, such as Tumblr, also enable the posting of images and longer text-based content.

Microblogs do not offer many of the community features found on larger social network sites. A microblog does not offer topic-based groups, one-to-one private messaging, photo sharing, and the like. The only service it offers is public message distribution.

The Tumblr microblogging service

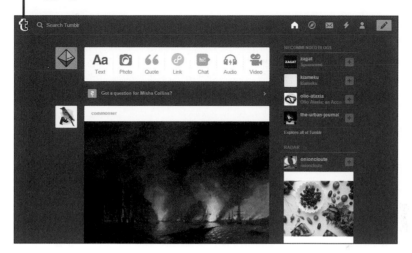

With a typical microblogging service, registered users post short text or messages or photos. Other users sign up to follow the posts of individual members; they are then notified when someone they follow makes a new post. Microblog posts are used to convey personal information and opinions; businesses also use them to make commercial announcements.

Many of the most-followed microbloggers are celebrities; fans follow their posts to learn more about the celebrities' activities. Major news organizations also use microblogs to post breaking stories, while individuals post details of their personal lives to interested friends and family followers.

The most popular microblogging services today include:

- Twitter (www.twitter.com)
- Tumblr (www.tumblr.com)

Message Boards

Many websites offer *online message boards* where users can interact by leaving their comments about particular articles or general topics. You can find message boards or comments sections on many general-interest and news-oriented sites, as well as on sites that focus on specific topics.

Message boards on the AARP website

A message board is a public forum. Users can start a new topic or comment on an existing one. Comments are organized into *threads*, with each successive user adding his comments to those comments left by previous users. It's not real-time interaction, but it is a continuing discussion.

The advantage of frequenting a given site's message board as opposed to using a larger, more general social network is that you know you're interacting with people who like the same things you do. Message boards create a community of like-minded users, not unlike a traditional club or group, but not limited by physical boundaries. If you're a model kit builder, for example, a kit building message board helps you keep in touch with kit builders from around the world.

Message Boards

Learn more about message boards in Chapter 15, "Getting Social on Special Interest Message Boards."

Social Bookmarking Services

The Reddit social bookmarking service

Finally, we have *social bookmarking services*, which represent a subset of the features found on a social network. A social bookmarking service lets users share their favorite websites and online articles with friends and colleagues online. A user visits a website, web page, news article, or blog post that he or she likes, and then clicks a button or link to bookmark that site. This bookmark then appears in his or her master list of bookmarks on the social bookmarking service site; the user can share all or some of these bookmarks with anyone he or she designates.

Most social bookmarking services use tags to help users find bookmarked sites. When a user bookmarks a site, he adds a few tags or keywords to describe the site. Other users can then search by keywords to find the most popular matching bookmarked sites—just as they search Google and the other traditional search engines.

Social bookmarking services are great ways to spread timely and interesting content. The most notable bookmarks on these sites quickly turn viral, as one user after another shares his or her links with other users.

In addition, the top social bookmarking services encourage conversations about the bookmarked items. In such a way are online communities created, built around the topic du jour.

The most popular social bookmarking vservices today include:

- Reddit (www.reddit.com)
- StumbleUpon (www.stumbleupon.com)

>>>*Go Further*

REDDIT

Reddit is the number-one social bookmarking service today, and actually goes well beyond that basic functionality. The Reddit site is a hotbed of lively online conversation between users—such a hotbed that the site generates a lot of controversy.

In fact, Reddit conversations are often so unruly—and sometimes vicious—that the site can be downright unfriendly to more genteel users. This is probably one reason why Reddit isn't widely used by older adults.

Discovering the Top Social Media for Older Users

Of all the various social media available today, which should you be interested in? The answer, as you might suspect, is that it all depends.

You need to choose your social media based on what you're interested in and who you want to stay in touch with. For example, if you just want to stay in touch with your cousin Emily and her family, or the neighbors from your old neighborhood, or the folks you go to church with, then a general social network such as Facebook is the right choice. If, on the other hand, you want to keep in contact with your old business associates, then LinkedIn's professional networking makes more sense. If you like to share pictures of recipes and do-it-yourself (DIY) projects, consider Pinterest. Or if you want to stay hip with what your younger children or grandchildren are up to, then the youth-oriented Twitter is the place to be.

That said, some social media have more appeal to older users than do others. The following graphic details the percentage of online users aged 50 to 64 who use various social media.

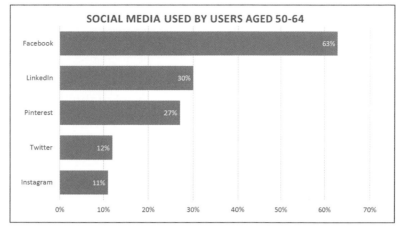

Statistics provided by the Pew Research Center's Internet Project, for the year 2014.

As you can see, Facebook is definitely the big dog among more mature users. If you only use one social medium, that's the one. But LinkedIn and Pinterest—and even Twitter and Instagram—also have appeal and might be worth considering. Let's a take a quick look at what each of these social media have to offer.

Facebook

There are lots of reasons why Facebook (www.facebook.com) is used by the majority of online users over 50. It's easy to use and doesn't require a lot of technical or computer expertise. It's big (more than 1 billion users), which means that most of your friends and family are already using it, so there are lots of people to interact with. And it offers a variety of features that help you connect or re-connect with people you know or used to know. In short, it's the whole ball of wax in a very user-friendly package.

People use Facebook to keep their friends informed of their latest activities, as well as to keep in touch with what their friends are doing. The average Facebook user has more than 300 friends on the site and spends more than seven hours per month connected to the Facebook site; the most obsessed users check in more than 20 times per day. (Older users tend to have fewer Facebook friends than do younger users; those aged 55 to 64 average 129 friends, for example.)

Because of its general nature, Facebook is popular among people of all ages. Users range from grade schoolers (actually, the minimum user age is 13) to retired snowbirds—with the older generation making up most of the site's growth in recent years.

In addition to posting and reading status updates, Facebook users have access to a variety of other community features. Facebook offers topic-oriented groups, pages for companies and celebrities, photo and video sharing, social games, instant text messages, and even one-to-one video chats. Many people log onto Facebook in the morning and stay logged in all day—there's that much to do there. And you can access all of Facebook's features from your computer, smartphone, or tablet.

In short, Facebook is the premier social medium for online users of all ages—and especially for those over age 50.

Facebook

Learn more about Facebook in Chapter 5, "Keeping in Touch with Friends and Family on Facebook."

LinkedIn

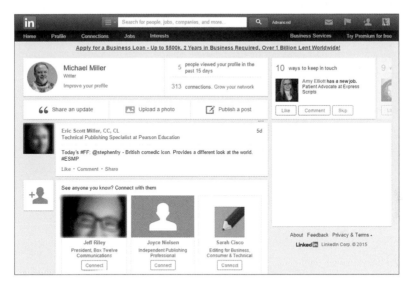

LinkedIn (www.linkedin.com) is a social network, like Facebook, but with a distinct focus on business. The site was launched in 2003 and currently has more than 364 million registered users.

LinkedIn is used primarily by business professionals, for networking and job hunting. It's a great place to keep in touch with current and former co-workers, as well as others in your profession.

More than a third of LinkedIn users are 50 years old and older. That's more than 100 million users aged 50 and up. Because of its professional focus, LinkedIn has a higher percentage of higher-income users than any other social media. Most LinkedIn users are successful in their chosen professions, with close to half describing themselves as "decision makers" in their companies.

In addition, millions of companies have LinkedIn Pages, in order to establish a strong industry presence. LinkedIn also counts among its members executives from all Fortune 500 companies.

People use LinkedIn to expand their list of business contacts, keep in touch with colleagues, give and receive professional endorsements, and keep abreast of developments in their profession. Contacts made on LinkedIn can be used for a number of different purposes, such as finding employment, making a sale, or exploring business opportunities. You can also use LinkedIn to gain an introduction to a specific individual you'd like to know, via connections with mutual contacts.

In short, if you're a business professional, LinkedIn needs to be part of your social media portfolio. Compared to other social media, this one is serious.

LinkedIn

Learn more about LinkedIn in Chapter 11, "Fine-Tuning Your Professional Profile on LinkedIn."

Pinterest

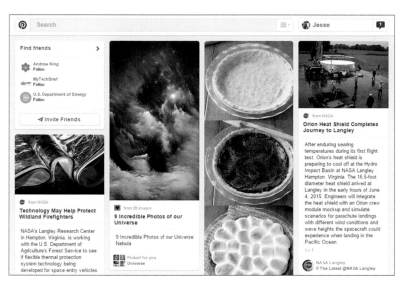

Pinterest (www.pinterest.com) is a fast-growing media sharing network. In a way, Pinterest is like Facebook but with only pictures. Members use Pinterest to share photos and other images they find interesting with their family and online friends.

The way it works is you find an image from a website or another user, and then you "pin" that image to one of your personal boards on the Pinterest site. Other users see what you've pinned, and if they like it, they *repin* it to their boards.

A Pinterest board is like an old-fashioned corkboard, only online. Your boards become places where you can create and share collections of those things you like or find interesting. You can have as many boards as you want, organized by category or topic. It's a way to collect images you like and share them with the wider Pinterest community.

Pinterest is unique among today's social media in that it has been strongly embraced by women of all ages. Fully 80% of Pinterest users are women, and almost a quarter are aged 50 and up. Pinterest users are more likely to live in Midwestern states instead of the coasts, and two-thirds are firmly middle-class.

The visual nature of Pinterest makes it attractive to non-technical users. It's the number-three social medium for older users, closely behind LinkedIn. If you're into collecting or recipes or DIY projects, Pinterest has a lot to offer.

Pinterest

Learn more about Pinterest in Chapters 9, "Pinning and Repinning on Pinterest" and 10, "Finding Other Users and Boards to Follow on Pinterest."

Twitter

Twitter (www.twitter.com) is a microblogging service particularly popular with people in their 20s and 30s. Users post short (140 character) text messages, called *tweets*, from their computers or mobile phones. Tweets are displayed to a user's followers and are searchable via the Twitter site.

Since its launch in 2006, Twitter has become the number-two social media site (after Facebook) and one of the top ten websites on the Internet. Twitter currently has more than 500 million users who generate an equal number of tweets each day. Only 16% of Twitter's users are over age 50, however; because it's a bit more technically difficult to use, it remains a social medium for younger users.

The lack of community features has also hindered Twitter's acceptance, especially among more mature users. It's a microblogging service, not a full-featured social network. With Twitter, you only get message posting and following; there's no photo sharing, instant messaging, or groups.

Given Twitter's limitations, why do younger people like it so much? Like Facebook, some people use Twitter to inform friends and family of what they're doing and thinking. Others use Twitter as a kind of personal blog, posting random thoughts and comments for all to read. Businesses use Twitter to promote their brands and products, making announcements via their Twitter feeds. Celebrities and entertainers (arguably the most-followed Tweeters) use their Twitter feeds as a kind of public relations (PR) channel, feeding information of their comings and goings to their fan bases. And news organizations use Twitter to disseminate the latest news headlines.

That last bit is important. While Twitter is not a formal news medium, in that it has no central organization or paid reporters, it has become an important medium for disseminating breaking news stories. Today, many major news stories are tweeted before they're announced by the traditional news media, either by individuals on the scene or by reporters who can quickly tweet about an event before filing a lengthier news report.

So if you want to keep abreast of breaking news (both actual and celebrity-related), or just want to see what the younger generation is up to, give Twitter a spin. Otherwise, a more fully-featured social network, such as Facebook, is probably a better choice.

Twitter

Learn more about Twitter in Chapter 13, "Tweeting and Retweeting on Twitter."

Instagram

Instagram (www.instagram.com) is a media sharing network based on a mobile app for Apple and Android phones. You use the Instagram app to take pictures with the camera in your phone, and then you post those pictures to the Instagram network. The pictures you post are viewed by your friends and followers, and then shared with their friends and followers.

While Instagram has a website, it's really mobile-based, as it relies on the pictures you take with your smartphone. In fact, some people use the Instagram app solely for taking pictures, as it offers a variety of filters and special effects to enhance the photos you take.

People use Instagram to document their lives, visually. When you do something of interest, you snap a picture and post it to Instagram. Your friends do the same. You don't need to read long, boring text posts, just look at pictures. There's an appeal to that—especially among younger users. To that end, 41% of Instagram's 300 million or so users are between the ages of 16 and 24; only 6% are between 50 and 64.

Instagram's users are quite active, posting more than 70 million photos a day. To date, users have shared more than 30 billion photos on Instagram, making it one of the top photo-sharing services on the Internet—even without the social component.

Instagram

Learn more about Instagram in Chapter 14, "Sharing Photos with Instagram."

In this chapter, you learn how to use Facebook, the Internet's largest social network.

→ Signing Up and Signing In
→ Finding Facebook Friends
→ Reading the News Feed
→ Posting Status Updates to Your Friends

Keeping in Touch with Friends and Family on Facebook

If you only join one social network, Facebook is the one. Facebook is the world's largest social network, a great place to keep in touch with family and friends wherever they live.

Signing Up and Signing In

When you're signed up as a Facebook member, you can post your own thoughts and comments, upload pictures to share, and even share your favorite web pages. Likewise, you can see what your friends and family are posting—their activities, photos, web links, and the like. That's why half of all online users aged 50 and up make Facebook their hub for online social activity—and check in at least an hour each day.

Create a New Facebook Account

To use Facebook, you first need to create a personal Facebook account. A Facebook account is free and easy to create; there's no fee to join and no monthly membership fees.

1. Use Internet Explorer, Microsoft Edge, Google Chrome, or any other web browser to go to Facebook's home page at www.facebook.com.

2. Go to the Sign Up section and enter your first name into the First Name box.

3. Enter your last name into the Last Name box.

4. Enter your email address into the Your Email box and then re-enter it into the Re-enter Email box.

5. Enter your desired password into the New Password box. Your password should be at least six characters in length—the longer the better, for security reasons.

6. Select your date of birth from the Birthday lists.

7. Check the appropriate option for your gender.

8. Click the Sign Up button.

Password Security

To make your password harder for hackers to guess, include a mix of alphabetic, numeric, and special characters, such as punctuation marks. You can also make your password more secure by making it longer; an eight-character password is much harder to crack than a six-character one. Just remember, though, that the more complex you make your password, the more difficult it may be for you to remember—which means you probably need to write it down somewhere, just in case. (And keep that written note hidden from prying eyes!)

>>>Go Further
EMAIL CONFIRMATION AND MORE

After you click the final Sign Up button, Facebook sends you an email message asking you to confirm your new Facebook account. When you receive this email, click the link to proceed.

You'll then be prompted to find friends who are already on Facebook, and to fill in a few personal details for your profile page. You can perform these tasks now or at a later time. (I prefer to save them until later, after I've configured Facebook's privacy settings—which we discuss in Chapter 8, "Configuring Facebook's Privacy Settings.")

Sign In to the Facebook Site

You use your email address and the password you created during the signup process to log in to your Facebook account. When you're logged in, Facebook displays your home page.

1. Use your web browser to go to Facebook's home page at www.facebook.com.

2. Enter your email address into the Email or Phone box.

3. Enter your password into the Password box.

4. Click the Log In button.

>>>Go Further

STAY LOGGED IN—OR NOT

If you don't want to enter your email and password every time you want to use the Facebook site, check the Keep Me Logged In option when you're signing in. This keeps your Facebook session open, even if you visit another website between Facebook pages.

You should not check the Keep Me Logged In option if you're using a public computer, such as one at the library, or if you share your computer with other users. Doing so makes it possible for other users to use your personal Facebook account, which you don't want. So if you share your PC or use a public computer, don't check the Keep Me Logged In option.

Sign Out of Your Facebook Account

You probably want to sign out of Facebook if you're not going to be active for an extended period of time. You also want to sign out if someone else in your household wants to access his or her Facebook account.

1. From any Facebook page, click the down arrow button at the far right side of the toolbar.

2. Click Log Out from the drop-down menu.

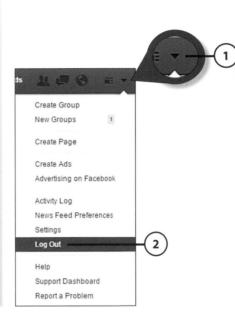

>>>Go Further
ABOUT FACEBOOK

Facebook is the brainchild of Mark Zuckerberg, an enterprising young man who came up with the concept while he was a student at Harvard in 2004. Facebook (called "thefacebook" at that time) was originally intended as a site where college students could socialize online. Sensing opportunity beyond the college market, Facebook opened its site to high school students in 2005 and then to all users over age 13 in 2006. Today, Facebook boasts more than 1 billion members worldwide.

Even though Facebook started out as a social network for college students, it isn't just for kids anymore. Today, fewer than 10% of Facebook users are college aged; a higher percentage (14%) are aged 55 or older. In fact, Facebook's strongest growth in the past few years has come from users over age 65. (Take that, you young whippersnappers!)

Why are older adults using Facebook? Most (40%) use Facebook to connect with family and old friends; 30% use Facebook to share digital photos; and 20% play social games on Facebook. That makes Facebook both useful and fun—a great combination for users of any age.

Finding Facebook Friends

Facebook is all about connecting with people you know. Anyone you connect with on Facebook is called a *friend*. A Facebook friend can be a real friend, or a family member, colleague, acquaintance—you name it. When you add someone to your Facebook friends list, he sees everything you post—and you see everything he posts.

Accept Facebook's Friend Suggestions

The easiest way to find friends on Facebook is to let Facebook find them for you based on the information you provided for your personal profile. The more Facebook knows about you, especially in terms of where you've lived, worked, and gone to school, the more friends it can find.

1. If you have a Find Friends button on the Facebook toolbar, click it. If not, click the Friends button to display the drop-down menu, and then click Find Friends.

2. This displays a page that lists any friend requests you've received and offers a number of friend suggestions from Facebook, in the People You May Know section. Keep scrolling down the page to view more friend suggestions.

Suggested Friends

The people Facebook suggests as friends are typically people who went to the same schools you did, worked at the same companies you did, or are friends of your current friends.

3. To invite a person to your friends list, click the Add Friend button next to that person's name.

Find Friends button — Find Friends

Lew   Home   Find Friends

Friend Requests   Find Friends · Settings

No new requests

No New Friend Requests
View Sent Requests

People You May Know

Marie Butler-Knight
Indiana University, Bloomington, IN   Add Friend

Paul Ray Breece
Works at I don't work for you, that's all you need to know   Add Friend

Anna Rendell
Works at DaySpring
Michael Miller is a mutual friend.   Add Friend

4. In the right column of the page, scroll down until you see the Search for Friends panel. To search for someone by name, enter that person's name into the Name box.

5. To search for people who are already friends with your other Facebook friends, go to the Mutual Friend section and check the names of one or more friends. (If a particular friend isn't listed, enter his or her name into the text box first.)

6. To look for people who come from your hometown, go to the Hometown section and check your town. (If your hometown isn't listed, enter it into the text box first.)

7. To search for people who live near you now, go to the Current City section and check your city. (If your town or city isn't listed, enter it into the text box first.)

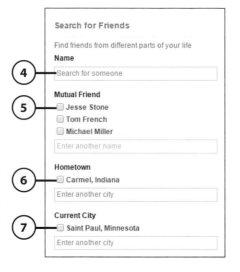

8. To search for people who went to the same high school you did, go to the High School section and check the name of your high school. (If your high school isn't listed, enter it into the text box first.)

9. To search for people who went to the same college or university you did, go to the College or University section and check the name of your school. (If your school isn't listed, enter its name into the text box first.)

10. To search for people who work or worked for one of your current or former employers, go to the Employer section and check the name of that company. (If a company isn't listed, enter its name into the text box first.)

11. To search for former classmates who went to the same graduate school you did (if, in fact, you went to graduate school), go to the Graduate School section and check the name of that school. (If your grad school isn't listed, enter its name into the text box first.)

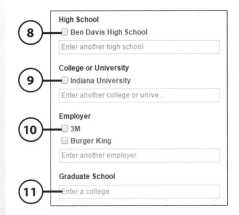

Multiple Filters

You can choose to filter your search on more than one criteria. For example, you can look for people who lived in your hometown and work at a given company, or who went to your college and live in your current city. Just select multiple options in the Search for Friends panel.

12. Whichever options you select, Facebook now returns a list of suggested friends based on your selection. Click the Add Friend button to send a friend request to a specific person.

>>>Go Further
INVITATIONS

When you click the Add Friend button, Facebook doesn't automatically add that person to your friends list. Instead, that person receives an invitation to be your friend; she can accept or reject the invitation. If a person accepts your request, you become friends with that person. If a person does not accept your request, you don't become friends (nor are you notified if your friend request is declined). In other words, you both have to agree to be friends—it's not a one-sided thing.

Find Email Contacts

Another way to find Facebook friends is to let Facebook look through your email contact lists for people who are also Facebook members. You can then invite those people to be your friends.

1. If you have a Find Friends button on the Facebook toolbar, click it. If not, click the Friends button to display the drop-down menu, and then click Find Friends.

2. On the top right side of the Friends page you see the Add Personal Contacts panel. Click the logo for the email service or contacts application you use—iCloud, Outlook.com/Hotmail, Yahoo! Mail, AOL Mail, Comcast, or Other Email Service.

3. Enter your email address and password, as requested.

4. Click the Find Friends button.

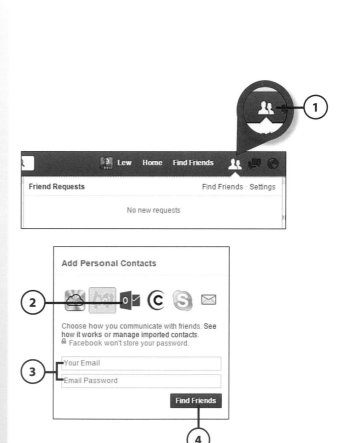

Sign In

At this point, you might be prompted to sign in to your email account or to link your email and Facebook accounts. Enter the required information to proceed.

5. Facebook displays a list of your email contacts who are also Facebook members. Check the box next to each person with whom you'd like to be friends.

6. Click the Add Friends button to send friend requests to these contacts, or click Skip to go to the next step.

7. You see a list of your other friends who are not yet Facebook members. Check the box next to each person you'd like to become a Facebook member (and join your friends list).

8. Click the Send Invites button.

Search for Old Friends

If Facebook doesn't automatically suggest a particular friend, there's still a good chance that person is already on Facebook and waiting for you to find him. It's your task to find that person—by searching the Facebook site.

1. Start to type a person's name into the Search box at the top of any Facebook page. As you type, Facebook displays a list of suggestions.

2. If your friend is listed, click the person's name to go to her Timeline (profile) page.

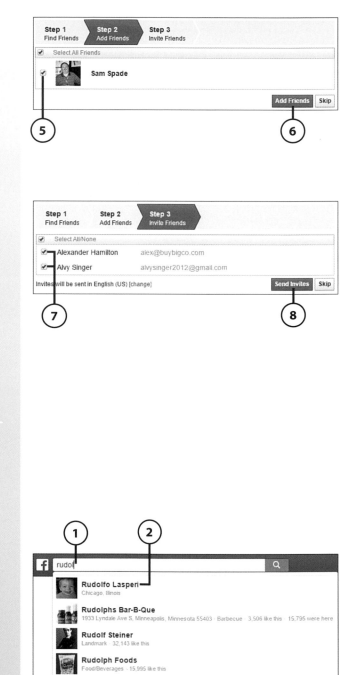

3. Click the Add Friend button to send an invitation to this person.

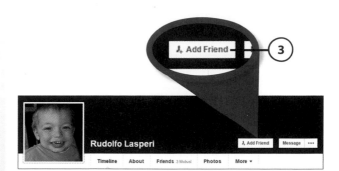

Accept a Friend Request

Sometimes potential Facebook friends find you before you find them. When this happens, they will send you a friend request, which you can then accept or decline. You might receive a friend request via email, or you can view friend requests within Facebook.

1. Click the Friend Request button on the Facebook toolbar. All pending friend requests are displayed in the drop-down menu.

2. Click Confirm to accept a specific friend request and be added to that person's friends list.

3. If you receive a request from someone you don't know (or someone you don't like), you can decline the request. Click Decline Request to decline the request.

No One Knows

When you decline a friend request, the sender is not notified by Facebook. That person doesn't know that you've declined the request, but just that you haven't (yet) accepted it. The same thing when you unfriend a friend; he or she is not notified when you sever the connection.

Unfriend a Friend

You can, at any time, remove any individual from your Facebook friends list. This is called *unfriending* the person, and it happens all the time.

1. Click your profile picture in the navigation sidebar or your name on the toolbar to display your Timeline page.

2. Click Friends beneath your name to display your Friends page.

3. Scroll to the person you want to unfriend and mouse over the Friends button to display the pop-up menu.

4. Select Unfriend.

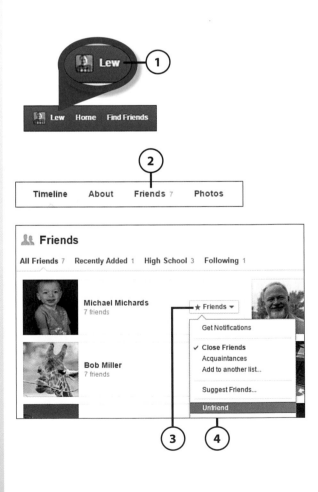

Reading the News Feed

Facebook's News Feed is where you keep abreast of what all your friends are up to. The News Feed consists of status updates made by your friends and by companies and celebrities you've liked on Facebook. It also includes posts from Facebook groups you've joined, as well as the occasional advertisement.

Display the News Feed

You can easily get to the News Feed from anywhere on the Facebook site, using the ever-present toolbar at the top of every Facebook page.

1. From the Facebook toolbar, click the Home button.

2. The News Feed displays in the center of the page. Note that in the navigation sidebar (left side menu), the top item, News Feed, is selected. If you later choose to display other content (by clicking an item in the sidebar), you can return to the News Feed by clicking News Feed in the sidebar.

3. The News Feed lists what Facebook deems to be your most relevant or interesting posts at the top. Scroll down to view additional posts.

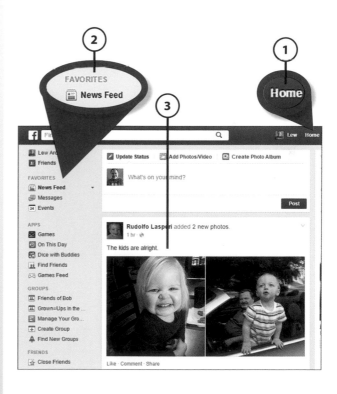

View a Status Update

Each status update in your News Feed consists of several distinct components.

1. The profile picture of the person who is posting (called the *poster*) appears in the top left corner.

2. The poster's name appears at the top of the post, beside the profile picture. To view more information about this person, mouse over his or her name; to view the poster's Timeline page, click the person's name.

3. When the item was posted is displayed beneath the poster's name.

4. The content of the status update appears under this top portion of the post. This can include text, images, or a video.

5. Links to like, comment on, and share this post appear after the post content.

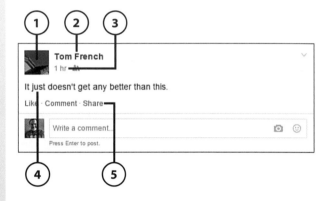

View Links to Web Pages

Many status updates include links to interesting web pages. You can click a link to view the web page posted by your friend.

1. The title of the linked-to web page appears under the normal status update text. Click the title to display the linked-to web page in a new tab of your web browser.

2. Many links include images from the linked-to page, as well as a short description of the page's content.

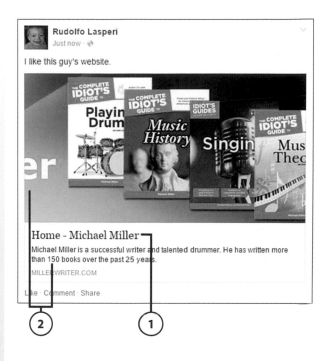

View Photos

It's common for Facebook users to post photos they've taken with their smartphones or digital cameras. These photos appear as part of the status update.

1. The photo appears in the body of the status update. (If more than one photo is posted, they may appear in a tiled collage or in a side-scrolling display.) To view a larger version of any picture, click the photo in the post.

2. This displays the photo within its own *lightbox*—a special window superimposed over the News Feed. To close the photo lightbox, click the X in the upper-right corner.

View Videos

Many Facebook users post their own home movies so their friends can view them. Other people like to share videos they find on YouTube and other video sharing sites.

1. A thumbnail image from the video appears in the body of the status update, with a "play" arrow superimposed on top of the image. Many videos start playing automatically when the post is viewed. For those that don't, click the image to play the video.

2. If the video plays with the sound muted, mouse over the video to display the playback controls and then click the Volume (speaker) button and adjust the volume.

3. To pause playback, mouse over the video and then click the Pause button.

4. To view the video full screen, click the full screen button.

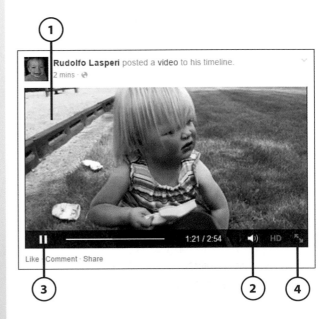

Like and Comment on an Update

Facebook is a social network, which means you can interact socially with the status updates your friends make. You can tell your friend you "like" a given post, you can comment on a post, and you can even share a post with other friends.

When you "like" a friend's status update, you give it a virtual "thumbs up." It's like voting on a post; when you view a status update, you see the number of "likes" that post has received.

1. To like an update, click Like. (Other people who have liked this status update are listed under the post.)

2. To comment on an update, type your comment into the Write a Comment box and press Enter. (If the Write a Comment box isn't displayed, click the Comment link.)

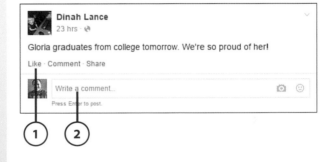

Share an Update

Occasionally, you'll find a status update that is interesting or intriguing enough you want to share it with all of your friends. You do this via Facebook's Share feature.

1. Click Share underneath the original post, and then click Share to display the Share This Status panel.

2. Enter any comments you might have on this post into the Say Something About This area.

3. Click the Share Status button to post the original status update and your newly added comments to your friends.

Posting Status Updates to Your Friends

To let your family and friends know what you've been up to, you need to post what Facebook calls a *status update*. Every status update you make is broadcast to everyone on your friends list, by being displayed in their News Feeds on their home pages. It's how they know what you've been doing and thinking about.

Post a Status Update

A status update is, at its most basic, a brief text message. It can be as short as a word or two, or it can be several paragraphs long; that's up to you. (Facebook lets you post updates with more than 60,000 characters, which should be more than long enough for most of us.)

1. Click the Home button on the Facebook toolbar to return to your home page.

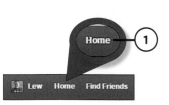

2. Go to the Publisher box (labeled What's On Your Mind?) at the top of the page. Note that the Update Status tab is selected by default.

3. Type your message into the What's On Your Mind? box. The Publisher box expands to display a series of option buttons at the bottom.

4. Click the Post button when you're done.

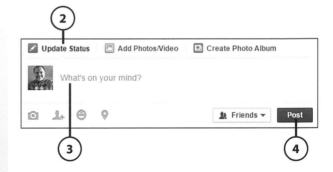

Post a Link to a Web Page

You can include links to other web pages in your status updates. Not only does Facebook add a link to the specified page, it also lets you include a thumbnail image from that page with the status update.

1. Start a new post as normal, and enter any accompanying text.

2. Enter the URL (web address) for the page you want to link to as part of your update.

3. Facebook should recognize the link and display a Link panel, complete with thumbnail image from the page. (If the web page doesn't include any pictures, you won't see a thumbnail image.) Click the left and right arrows to select one of multiple thumbnail images to accompany the link.

4. If you don't want to display an image from the page, click the X in the top right corner of the thumbnail image.

5. Click the Post button when done.

Post a Photograph or Video

Facebook enables you to embed digital photographs and videos in your posts. It's the Facebook equivalent of attaching a file to an email message.

1. Go to the Publisher box and click Add Photos/Video; this displays the Choose File to Upload or Open dialog box. (Which dialog box displays depends on which web browser you're using.)

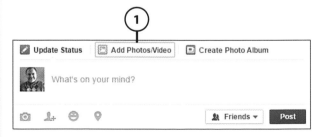

2. Navigate to and select the photo or video file(s) you want to upload. You can upload a single video file or multiple photo files; to select more than one file, hold down the Ctrl key while you click each filename.

3. Click the Open button.

4. You're returned to the Publisher box with your photo(s) added. Click the + icon to add another picture, if you want.

5. If you like, enter a short text message describing the photo(s) or video.

6. Click the Post button.

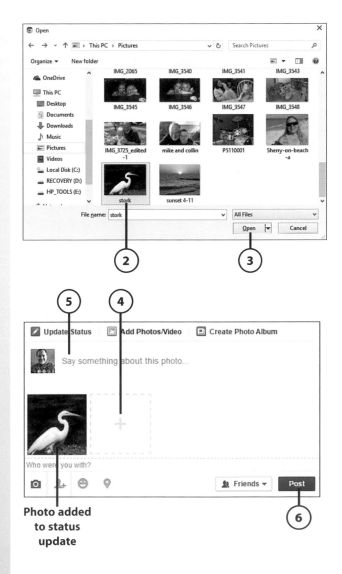

Photo added
to status
update

Add Your Location to a Post

Facebook enables you to identify your current location in any post you make. This lets your friends know where you are at any given time.

1. Enter the text of your status update into the Publisher box as you normally would, or select any photos you want to post.

2. Click the Add a Location to Post button beneath the Publisher box.

3. If Facebook can tell your location automatically, it displays a list of options. Otherwise, start entering your location manually; as you type, Facebook displays a list of suggested locations, along with a map of the current selection.

4. Click the correct location from the resulting list.

5. Click the Post button.

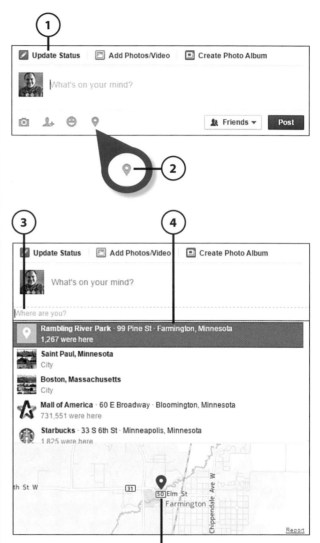

Map of selected location

Location added to post

It's Not All Good

Don't Publicize Your Location

You might not want to identify your location on every post you make. If you post while you're away from home, you're letting potential burglars know that your house is empty. You're also telling potential stalkers where they can find you. For these reasons, use caution when posting your location in your status updates.

Tag a Friend in a Post

Sometimes you might want to mention one of your friends in a status update, or include a friend who was with you when the post was made. You can do this by "tagging" friends in your status updates; the resulting post includes a link to the tagged person or persons.

Tags

A *tag* is a way to mention other Facebook users in your status updates and photos. When a person is tagged in a post, that post appears in that person's Facebook News Feed, so he knows you're talking about him. In addition, readers can click a tagged name to display that person's Timeline page.

1. Enter the text of your status update into the Publisher box as you normally would, or any photos you want to post.

2. Click the Tag People in Your Post button beneath the Publisher box.

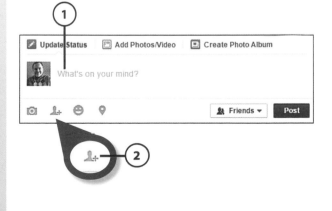

3. Enter the name of the person you want to tag. As you type, Facebook displays a drop-down list with matching names from your Facebook friends list.

4. Select the friend from the list.

5. Click the Post button.

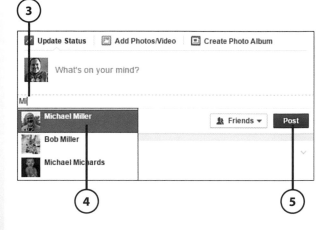

Determine Who Can— or Can't—See a Status Update

You can configure Facebook so that everyone on the site can read every post you make. If you'd rather send a given post to a more select group of people, you can change the privacy settings for any individual post. This enables only selected people to see that post; other people on your friends list won't see it at all.

1. Enter the text of your status update, or any photos you want to upload, into the Publisher box as normal.

2. Click the Privacy button (the second button from the right beneath the post) to display a list of privacy options.

3. Click Public to let everyone on Facebook see the post.

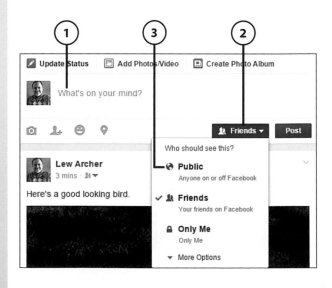

4. Select Friends to make a post visible only to people on your friends list.

5. Click Only Me to make the post only visible to yourself—no one else will be able to see it.

6. Click More Options to view more privacy options.

7. In the bottom section of the menu list, click the name of a specific friends list to make a post visible only to the friends on that list.

8. To select specific individuals who can or can't view this post, click Custom; this displays the Custom Privacy panel.

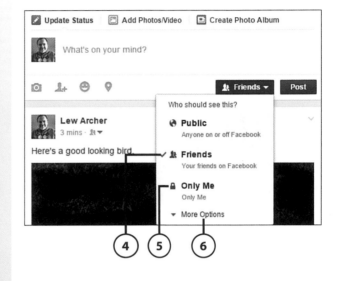

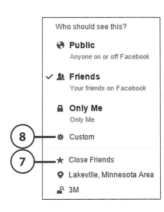

9. Go to the Share With section and make a selection from the These People or Lists list to make this post visible to specific friends, friends lists, or networks.

10. To hide this post from specific friends or friends lists, go to the Don't Share This With section and enter names into the These People or Lists box.

11. Click the Save Changes button.

12. Back in your post, click the Post button to send this status update to those people you've selected.

Configure Privacy for All Your Posts

Although you can configure the privacy option for each post you make individually, you can also set universal privacy settings that affect all your status updates. Learn more in Chapter 8.

Custom Privacy ×

+ **Share with**

These people or lists   [Friends ×]

Friends of tagged   ✔

Note: Anyone tagged can also see this post.

× **Don't share with**

These people or lists   [   ]

[Cancel] [**Save Changes**]

(10) (9) (11)

[👥 Friends ▾] [**Post**]

(12)

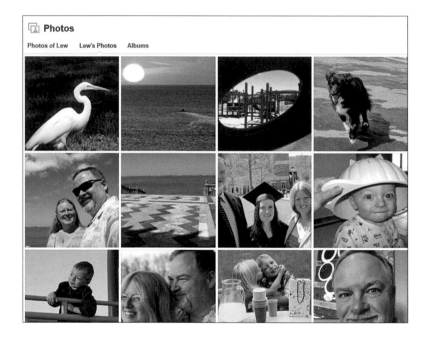

6

Sharing Pictures and Videos on Facebook

Before everybody got on the Internet, if you wanted to share photos with your family or friends, you had to make prints and mail them out to everyone, or invite everybody over to your house for an old-fashioned slide show. Today, however, you can share your photos online—via Facebook.

And Facebook is also a great place to share any home movies you've taken with your smartphone or camcorder. It's easy to upload photos and videos to Facebook and then share them with all your Facebook friends. Not surprisingly, it's equally easy to view your friends' photos and videos on Facebook.

Viewing Friends' Photos and Videos

Some people on Facebook post photos and videos as part of their regular status updates. These photos appear in your News Feed, as part of the stream of your friends' status updates.

Other Facebook users post photos to special photo albums they've created in their Facebook accounts. This is a more serious and organized way to share a large number of photos online. You can view these photo albums from the user's Timeline page.

View Photos in Your News Feed

When a friend posts a photo as part of a status update, that photo appears in your News Feed. You can view photos at that small size within the News Feed, or enlarge them to view them full screen.

1. Within your News Feed, all photos appear within the bodies of the accompanying status updates. To view a larger version of any picture, click the photo in the post. This displays the photo within its own *lightbox*—a special window superimposed over the News Feed.

2. To display various options (for tagging people, downloading photos, and so forth), mouse over the photo to display the bottom menu bar.

3. To close the photo viewer, click the X in the upper-right corner.

View Videos in Your News Feed

Viewing videos on Facebook is similar to viewing photos. When one of your friends uploads a video to Facebook, it shows up in your News Feed as a thumbnail image with a playback arrow on top. Playing a video is as easy as clicking that image.

1. Navigate to the status update that contains the video and then click the video thumbnail to play the video. (In some cases, the video will play automatically when you scroll to the post, but without sound—kind of like a muted preview. You'll need to click the video to play it back with sound.)

2. If you want to view the video at a larger size, mouse over the video to display the playback controls at the bottom, and then click the Full Screen icon at the lower-right corner. Click Esc (Escape) on your computer keyboard to return to normal playback mode.

3. To pause the playback, mouse over the video to display the playback controls and then click the Pause button; the button changes to a Play button. Click the Play button to resume playback.

4. Click and drag the volume control to raise or lower the playback volume.

5. Click and drag the time slider to move to another point in the video.

YouTube Videos

If someone has posted a video from YouTube, Vimeo, or another video-sharing site, playback will probably take place within the News Feed. To view the video on the YouTube or Vimeo site, click the title of the video to open that site in a new tab in your web browser.

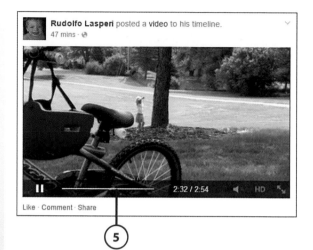

View All of a Friend's Photos and Videos

More serious photographers—and those people with lots of photos to share—organize their Facebook photos into separate photo albums. These are virtual versions of those traditional photo albums you've kept in the past. You can then navigate through a friend's photo albums to find and view the photos you like.

All the videos a friend uploads are stored in a special photo album labeled Videos. You can play back any video from there.

1. Click your friend's name or profile picture anywhere on Facebook to open his Timeline page.

2. Click Photos under the person's cover photo to display your friend's Photos page.

3. Click Photos of *Friend* to view individual photos of your friend.

4. Click *Friend's* Photos to view all photos posted by your friend.

5. Click Albums to view photos as posted in their photo albums.

6. Click to open the selected album. (Videos are located in the Videos album.)

7. Click the thumbnail of the picture you want to view. Facebook displays the selected picture in a lightbox superimposed on top of the previous page.

8. For videos, click the thumbnail of the video you want to play. Facebook plays the video on a separate video playback page.

Share a Photo or Video

If you really like a given photo or video, you can share that item on your own Timeline—with your own description.

1. Display the photo or video and click the Share link; this displays the Share This Photo or Share This Video panel.

2. Enter a description of the photo into the Say Something About This box.

3. Click the Privacy button and select who can view this photo: Public, Friends, Only Me, or Custom.

4. Click the Share Photo or Share Video button to post this item to your timeline.

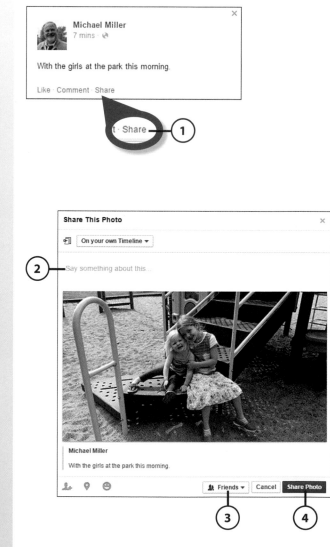

Download a Photo

If you find a friend's photo that you really like, you can download it to your own computer, for your own use.

1. Display the photo and mouse over the photo to display the menu at the bottom of the photo.

2. Click Options, and then click Download.

3. Click Save if you're prompted to open or save the file.

4. If you see the Save As dialog box, select where you want to save the file, and then click the Save button.

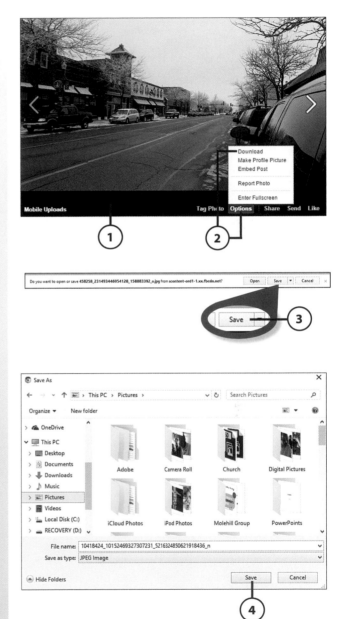

Sharing Your Own Photos and Videos with Friends

It seems like just about everybody these days has a digital camera, or a camera built into his smartphone or tablet. That means we're taking a lot more pictures than ever before—and those pictures can be shared with friends and family on Facebook.

The first thing you need to do is transfer your photos from your camera or phone to your computer. Then it's relatively easy to upload and share your own pictures on the Facebook site. You can upload new photos to an existing photo album or create a new album for newly uploaded photos.

>>>*Go Further*

POSTING PHOTOS FROM YOUR PHONE

If you use your cell phone to take photos, it's even easier to post those photos to Facebook. You don't have to transfer your phone photos to your PC first (although you can); Facebook lets you upload photos directly from your smartphone, using Facebook's mobile app.

With most smartphones today, Facebook uploading is built into the phone's operating system. Just open your phone's photo gallery or app and then open the photo you want to upload. Tap the Share icon and then tap the Facebook icon. When prompted, enter some text to go along with the photo, add location information if you like, and select the privacy level for this post. When you're ready, tap the Post button and the selected photo is posted to your Facebook feed.

Upload Photos to a New Photo Album

If you have a lot of photos to share on Facebook, the best approach is to create a series of virtual photo albums. This enables you to organize your photos by topic or date. For example, you might create an album for European Vacation, Christmas 2014, Grandkids, or Retirement Party. Organizing your photos into albums also makes it easier for your friends to find specific photos.

1. Click your name in the Facebook toolbar to display your Timeline page.

2. Underneath the cover photo at the top of the page, click Photos to display your Photos page.

3. Click the Create Album button to display the Open dialog box.

4. Select the photo(s) you want to upload.

5. Click the Open button to see the Untitled Album page.

Selecting Multiple Photos

You can upload more than one photo at a time. Hold down the Ctrl key while clicking files to select multiple files.

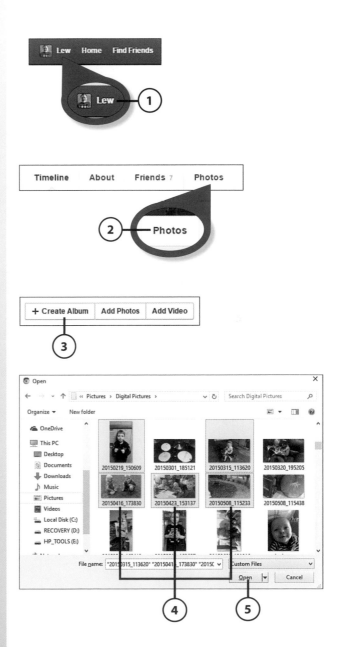

6. Click Untitled Album and enter the desired album title.

7. Click Say Something About This Album and enter an album description.

Optional Information

All the information you can add to a photo album is entirely optional; you can add as much or as little as you like. You don't even have to add a title—if you don't, Facebook uses the title Untitled Album.

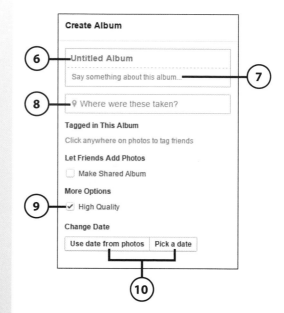

8. Enter a location in the Where Were These Taken? box to enter a geographic location for all the photos in this album.

9. To upload photos at the highest possible quality, check the High Quality option.

10. In the Change Date section, click either Use Date from Photos (to use exact dates for each photo) or Pick a Date (to assign all photos the same date).

High-Quality Photos

For the best possible picture for anyone downloading or printing your photos, check the High Quality option to upload and store your photos at their original resolution. Note, however, that it takes longer to upload high-quality photos than those in standard quality.

11. To enter information about a specific picture, enter a description in the Say Something About This Photo box for that photo.

12. To tag a person in a given photo, click that person's face and enter his or her name when prompted.

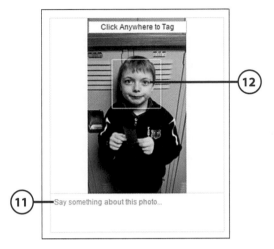

Photo Tagging

You identify people in your photos by *tagging* them. That is, you click a person in the photo and then assign a friend's name to that part of the photo. You can then find photos where a given person appears by searching for that person's tag.

13. Click the Privacy button and make a selection—Public, Friends, Only Me, or Custom— to determine who can view the photos in this album.

14. Click the Post button.

Upload Photos to an Existing Photo Album

After you've created a photo album, you can easily upload more photos to that album.

1. Open your Timeline page and then click Photos to display your Photos page.

2. Click Albums to display your existing photo albums.

3. Click the album you want to add new photos to.

4. When the album page opens, click the Add Photos tile to display the Open dialog box.

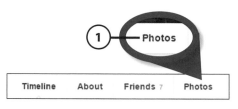

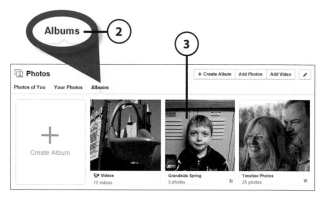

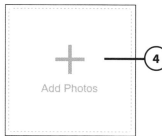

5. Navigate to and select the photo(s) to upload.

6. Click the Open button.

7. When the next page appears, you see the new photo(s) you've chosen to upload. Enter a description for each picture in the Say Something About This Photo box.

8. To tag a person who appears in a photo, click that person's face and enter his or her name.

9. Click the Post button. The new photos are now added to the existing album.

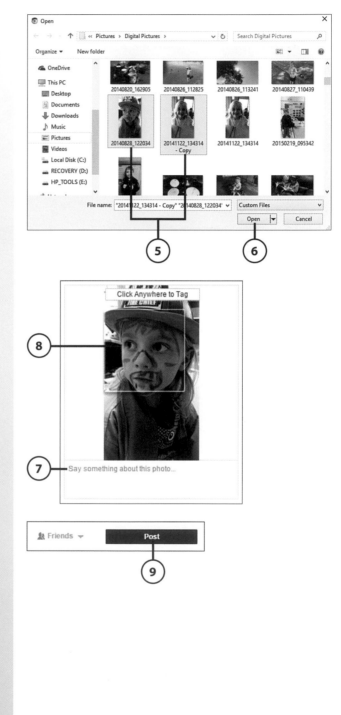

Upload a Video

If you shoot your own home videos, you can share them with friends and family by uploading them to Facebook. Facebook lets you upload just about any type of video to your Videos album, accessible from your Timeline for all your friends to view.

Video Restrictions

When uploading videos to Facebook, the video files must be no more than 20 minutes long and no more than 1024MB (approximately 1GB) in size. Facebook accepts videos in all major video file formats, including high-definition videos.

1. Open your Timeline page and click Photos to open your Photos page.

2. Click the Add Video button to display the Upload Video panel.

3. Click the Choose File button to display the Choose File to Upload or Open dialog box.

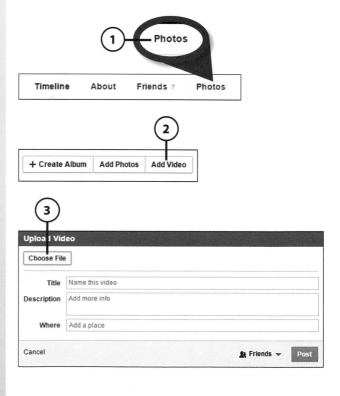

4. Navigate to and select the video file you want to upload.

5. Click the Open button to return to the Upload Video panel.

6. Enter a title for the video into the Title box.

7. Enter a short description of the video into the Description box.

8. Enter a location in the Where box to specify where the video was taken.

9. Click the Privacy button and select who can view this video: Public, Friends, or Custom.

10. Click the Post button when done.

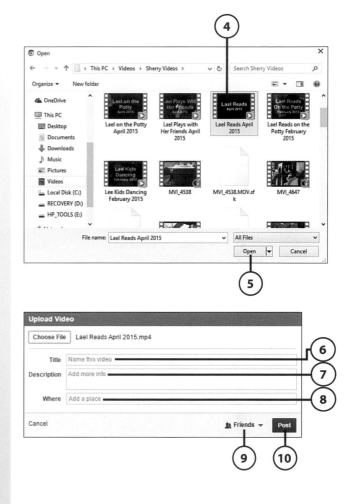

Processing

After a video is uploaded, Facebook must process it into the proper format to distribute on its site. This might take several minutes. You should be informed when the processing is complete; you can then edit the video description if you like, or select a thumbnail image for the video.

Suggested Groups   Friends' Groups   Local Groups   **Your Groups**   + Create Group

GROUPS YOU'RE IN

Growing up on the Indy westside!   + Add to Favorites   ⚙

Kaitlyn's Kloset - MN   + Add to Favorites   ⚙

You Grew Up in (around) Indianapolis If...   + Add to Favorites   ⚙

Ben Davis - Where is *and/or* Do you remember   ✓ Added to Favorites ⚙

Ben Davis High School Class of 1975   ✓ Added to Favorites ⚙

Old Time Indy's long missed businesses, and forgotten history.   ✓ Added to Favorites ⚙

CED Magic - the RCA Selectavision Video Disc 20+   + Add to Favorites   ⚙

Fibes Drums 17   ✓ Added to Favorites ⚙

Hal Blaine   + Add to Favorites   ⚙

The Sense of Humor Club 20+   + Add to Favorites   ⚙

Grew Up in Eagledale 20+   ✓ Added to Favorites ⚙

The Great Drummer's Group 20+   + Add to Favorites   ⚙

Ludwig vintage snares and drums 20+   + Add to Favorites   ⚙

Discovering Interesting Groups on Facebook

If you want to make new friends—and reconnect with old ones—one of the best ways to do so is to search out others who share your interests. If you're into gardening, look for gardeners. If you're into recreational vehicles, look for fellow RVers. If you're a wine lover, look for other connoisseurs of the grape.

Even better, look for people who've shared your life experiences. That means connecting with people who went to the same schools, lived in the same neighborhoods, and participated in the same activities.

You can find people who share your history and hobbies in Facebook *groups*. A group takes the form of a special Facebook page, a place for people interested in that topic to meet online and exchange information and pleasantries.

Participating in Facebook Groups

A Facebook group is a special page devoted to a particular topic. You can find groups for various sports, hobbies, and activities, as well as those devoted to particular times and places, such as your old neighborhood when you were a kid.

Search for Groups

Facebook offers tens of thousands of different groups online, so chances are you can find one or more that suit you. The key is finding a particular group that matches what you're interested in—which you do by searching.

1. Go to the Search box in the Facebook toolbar and enter one or more keywords that describe what you're looking for. For example, if you're interested in golfing, enter **golf**. If you're looking for a group for the class of 1965, enter **class of 1965**. If you want to find a group created by people who live on the west side of Indianapolis, enter **Indianapolis west side**.

2. As you type, Facebook displays a list of items that match your query. If you see an interesting group in this list, click it.

3. If you don't see any matching groups in this short list, continue typing your query and press Enter to display a search results page.

4. Click More and then select Groups to display related groups.

5. To view a group's Facebook page, click the name of the group.

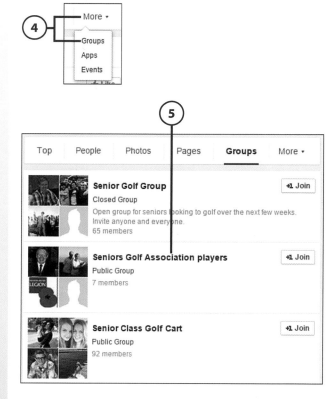

Browse for and Join Groups

There are also several ways to browse for Facebook groups—by following Facebook's suggestions, exploring groups that your friends belong to, and viewing groups for your local area.

1. On Facebook's Home page, scroll down the navigation sidebar to the Groups section and click More. This displays the Groups page.

2. Click the Suggested Groups tab to display those groups in which Facebook thinks you might be interested.

3. Click the Friends' Groups tab to view groups that your Facebook friends have joined.

4. Click the Local Groups tab to view groups located in your area, such as those for local schools, organizations, and towns.

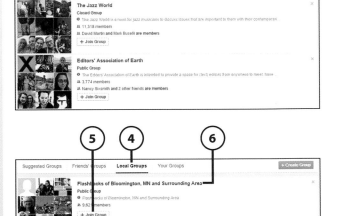

5. To join the group from this page, click the Join Group button.

6. To learn more about a group, click the group's name.

7. From the group's page, click the Join Group button to join this group.

>>>Go Further

PUBLIC AND CLOSED GROUPS

Most groups are classified as Public groups, meaning they're open for all Facebook members to join. Some groups, however, are Closed groups, which require that the group administrator approve all requests for membership.

To join a Closed group, you must apply for membership, and hope that your request is granted. When you click the Join button, a request goes to the group administrator. If your request is granted, you receive a message that you've been approved and are now an official member of the group. If your request is not granted, you don't get any response.

Visit a Group Page

Although you can view a feed of messages from all your groups (covered later in this chapter), most people prefer to visit individual group pages. This enables you to partake in all of the resources available in a given group.

1. On Facebook's Home page, scroll down the navigation sidebar to the Groups section and click More. This displays the Groups page with the Your Groups tab selected.

2. Scroll down to the Groups You're In section, and then click the name of a group to open its Facebook page.

3. All posts from members are displayed in the scrolling feed in the middle of the page. Click Like to like a particular post, Comment to reply to a post, or Share to share a post on your News Feed.

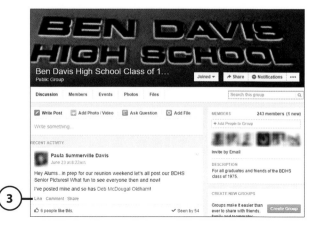

Post a New Message

Not only can you reply to posts made by other members, you can start a new discussion by posting a new message on the group's page. Other group members can then like and reply to your message.

1. Open the group's page, scroll to the Publisher box, and click Write Post.

2. Enter your message into the Write Something box; this expands the box.

3. Click the Tag People in Your Post button to tag another friend in this post.

4. Click the Add a Location to Post button to add a location to this post.

5. Click the Add Photos to Your Post (camera icon) button to add one or more photographs to this post.

6. Click the Post button to post your message to the group.

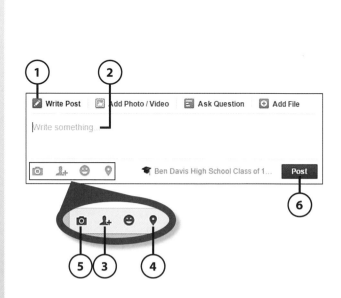

View Group Members

Who belongs to this particular group? It's easy to view all the members of a Facebook group.

1. Open the group's page and click Members to display a list of group members.

2. To search for a particular member, enter that person's name into the Find a Member box and press Enter.

3. Mouse over a member's name to view more information about that person.

4. To add a group member as a friend, click Add Friend.

5. To view a person's Timeline profile page, click that member's name.

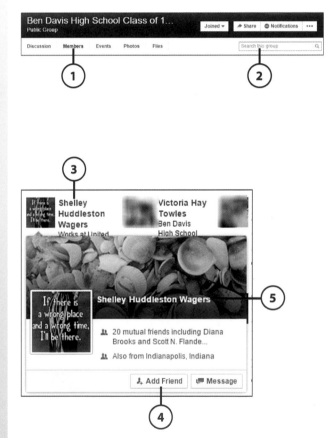

View Group Photos

Most groups let members post photos (and, in some cases, videos) of interest to other group members. If you're a member of a crafts group, for example, members might post photos of projects they've created. If you're a member of a group of old high school friends, members might post old photos from your school days. Viewing group photos, then, can be a fun activity.

1. Open the group's page and click Photos to display a list of group photos and photo albums.

2. Click a photo album to view all the photos in that album.

3. Click an individual photo to view that photo in a larger lightbox.

Upload Photos to the Group

You can upload your own photos to a group. This is a great way to share your activities with other group members.

1. Open the group's page and click Photos to display the group photos page.

2. Open the album to which you want to upload your photos.

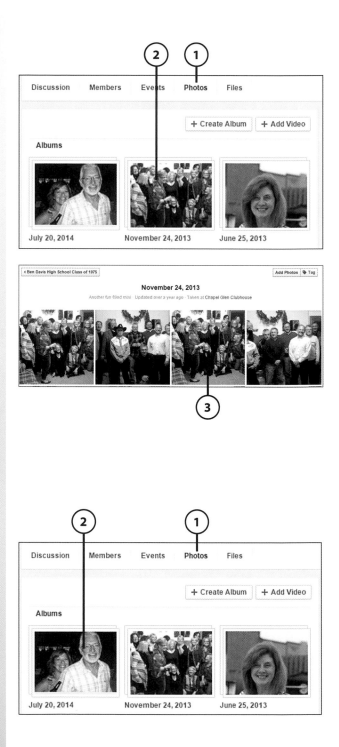

3. Click Add Photos to display the Choose Files to Upload or Open dialog box.

4. Select the photo or photos you want to upload.

5. Click the Open button.

6. Enter a short description of the photo into the Say Something About This Photo box.

7. Click any person's face to tag a person in this photo.

8. Click the Where Were These Taken? box to enter the location of this photo.

9. Click the Post button to add these photos to the group.

Uploading Videos

You can also upload your own videos to a group. Go to the main photos page, click the Upload Video button, and proceed from there.

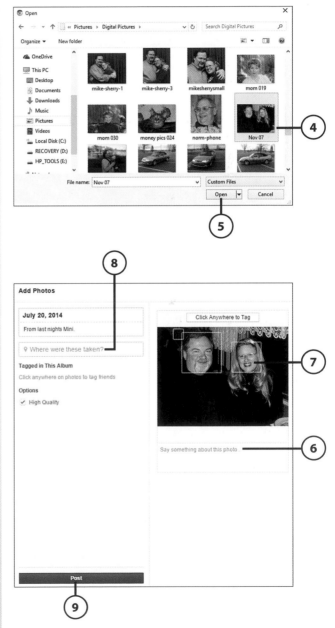

Get Notified of Group Activity

If you're active in a Facebook group, you might want to be notified when others post to the group. You can opt to receive notifications of each post made, or only of those posts made by your friends.

1. Open the group's page and click Notifications.

2. To receive a notification whenever a post is made to the group, select All Posts.

3. To receive notification of the most important posts, select Highlights.

4. To receive a notification whenever one of your Facebook friends posts to this group, select Friends' Posts.

5. To receive no notifications from this group, select Off.

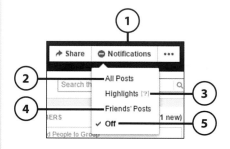

Leave a Group

If you grow tired of irrelevant or uninteresting posts in a given group, you can choose to unsubscribe from or leave a group.

1. On Facebook's Home page, scroll down the navigation sidebar to the Groups section and click More. This displays the Groups page with the Your Groups tab selected.

2. Scroll down to the Groups You're In section and find the group you want to leave.

3. Click the gear button for that group and then click Leave Group.

4. In the next dialog box, check the Prevent Other Members from Adding You Back to This Group option.

5. Click the Leave Group button.

② 2

| Grew Up In Eagledale |
| Advocates for "It's a Mad Mad Mad Mad World" (1963) |
| Old Time Indy's long missed businesses, and forgotten history. |

③ 3

✓ Added to Favorites
Edit Notification Settings
Leave Group
✓ Added to Favorites

Leave this Group? ✕

Do you want to leave Grew Up In Eagledale? You can also report this group.

☐ Prevent other members from adding you back to this group   Cancel **Leave Group**

④ 4

⑤ 5

>>>Go Further

USING GROUPS TO RECONNECT WITH OLD FRIENDS

On the surface, it's easy to think of Facebook groups as 21st-century versions of the homeroom clubs you had back in high school. You know, chess club, knitting club, model airplane club, and the like.

While there certainly are a huge number of these club-like Facebook groups, there are also groups that are more about times and places than they are about hobbies and interests. As such, these groups attempt to reconnect people with shared experiences.

I belong to a number of groups that connect me back to the days of my youth. For example, I grew up on the west side of Indianapolis, and there's a Facebook group called Growing Up on Indy's Westside to which I belong. It's a fun little group, with people posting faded pictures of old haunts, and lots of discussions about the way things used to be and what we used to do back then. I can't say I contribute too often, but it's always fun to read what others post.

I also belong to a "Where is and/or who do you remember?" group for my high school. This is a great place to find out what my old classmates have been up to in the decades since graduation. There are lots of posts asking about individual students, teachers, and events. It's a nice stroll down memory lane.

The point is, participating in Facebook groups can be a great way to reconnect with your past. You might even meet up with some of your old friends in these groups, or make some new friends you should have made way back then. It's kind of a virtual blast from the past, and we have the Facebook social network to thank for it.

Following Companies and Celebrities on Facebook

Even though businesses, celebrities, and public figures aren't regular users, they still want to use Facebook to connect with their customers and fans. They do this through their own Facebook Pages. If you're a customer or fan of a given company or celebrity, you can "like" that entity's Facebook page—and keep abreast of what that company or individual is up to. It's kind of like joining an online fan club through Facebook.

Search for Companies and Celebrities

Many companies and organizations have Facebook Pages for their brands and the products they sell. For example, you can find and follow Pages for Walmart, Starbucks, McDonalds, and AARP on Facebook.

Many famous people—entertainers, athletes, news reporters, politicians, and the like—also have Facebook Pages. So if you're a fan of James Taylor, Tom Hanks, Jack Nicklaus, or Bill O'Reilly, you can follow any or all of them via their Facebook Pages.

1. Enter one or more keywords that describe the person, company, or organization into the Search box on the Facebook toolbar. As you type, Facebook displays a list of pages and people that match your query.

2. If the Page you want is listed, click it.

3. If the Page you want is not listed, continue typing, and then press Enter to display a list of pages that match your query.

Local Pages

Facebook Pages aren't reserved for big public companies and celebrities. Many cities, libraries, schools, and even neighborhood associations have their own Facebook Pages. You can often find local events and discounts by visiting these local Pages.

View a Facebook Page

A professional Facebook Page is very similar to a personal Timeline page, right down to the timeline of updates and activities. Pages can feature specialized content, however, which is located at the top of the page, under the cover image. For example, a musician's page might feature an audio player for that performer's songs; other pages might let you view pictures and videos, or even purchase items online.

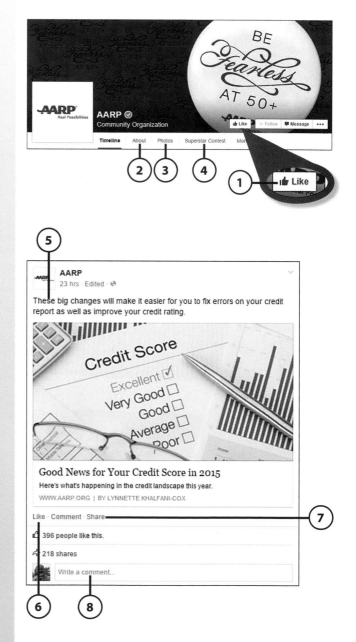

1. Click the Like button to like (follow) this page.

2. Click About to read more about this person or organization.

3. Click Photos to view the Page's official pictures.

4. Click any other content to view that content.

5. Scroll down to view status updates and other postings.

6. Click Like to like a specific post.

7. Click Share to share a post on your News Feed.

8. Click Comment and then type into the Comment box to leave a comment on a specific post.

View Page Posts in Your Pages Feed

Obviously, you can visit a company's' or celebrity's Facebook Page to view the latest updates and content. You can also view updates from all the Pages you like in Facebook's Pages Feed, which is fairly well hidden in the navigation sidebar. The Pages Feed is kind of like a News Feed for the Pages you've liked, not for the individuals you're friends with.

1. On the Facebook toolbar, click Home to display your Home page.

2. On your Home page, scroll down the navigation sidebar to the Pages section.

3. Click Pages Feed to display the Pages Feed in place of the normal News Feed.

4. Posts from all the Pages you follow are listed in the Pages Feed, newest first. Scroll down to view more posts.

5. Click Like to like a status update.

6. Click Share to share a post on your News Feed.

7. Click Comment and type into the Comment box to comment on an update.

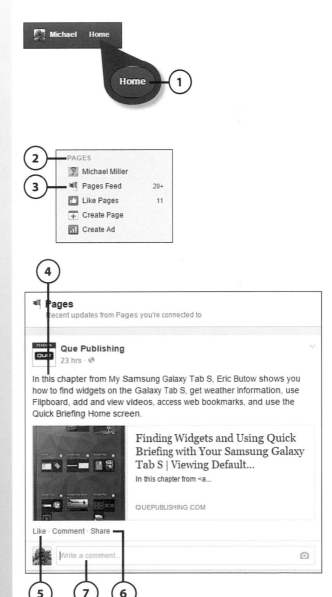

8. To return to the normal News Feed, click News Feed in the Favorites section of the navigation sidebar.

>>>Go Further

PROMOTED VERSUS ORGANIC POSTS

Facebook used to display all posts from those Pages you like in your News Feed. It doesn't do that anymore. That's because Facebook is in the business of making money, and one way it does that is to charge companies to "promote" their Page posts.

When a post is promoted (that is, paid for), Facebook will display it in the News Feeds of all that page's followers. If a post is not promoted, Facebook probably won't display that post. If a company wants its followers to see its posts, it pretty much has to pay for that privilege.

While some non-promoted posts may show up in your News Feed from time to time, Facebook displays less than 20% of a Page's "organic" (non-paid) posts. In other words, "liking" a given Page does not guarantee that you'll see all (or even most) of the posts to that Page. If you want to see all that a company or person is posting, you have to go to that Page to read the posts directly—or view your Pages Feed, as just discussed.

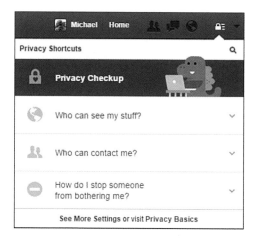

In this chapter, you learn how to protect your personal information by configuring Facebook's privacy settings.

→ Determining Who Sees What You Post
→ Limiting Contact from Other Members
→ Controlling Tagging
→ Managing Who Sees What on Your Timeline

Configuring Facebook's Privacy Settings

Social media are *social* media, which means they're all about sharing one's personal information with others. If you'd rather not share everything with everybody—if you want to keep some private things private—then you need to configure the privacy settings for each social media network you use.

You learned the basics of social media privacy in Chapter 3, "Using Social Media—Safely and Privately." Since Facebook is the world's largest social network, and the one most used by those over age 50, it's worth exploring Facebook's various privacy settings. Configuring these settings is essential if you don't want all your personal information made public.

Determining Who Sees What You Post

Many people worry about their privacy online, and for good reason. Not only are there a lot of companies that would like to get hold of your private information to contact you for advertising and promotional reasons, the Internet is also rife with identify thieves eager to steal your private information for their own nefarious means.

This is why many older users are cautious about getting on Facebook; they're afraid that the information they post will be needlessly shared with the wrong people. There's a basis to these fears, as Facebook likes to share all your information with just about everybody on its social network—not just your friends or their friends, but also advertisers and third-party websites.

Fortunately, you can configure Facebook to be much less public than it could be—and thus keep your private information private. You just have to know which settings to tweak.

Configure Facebook's Default Privacy Settings

The first step to ensuring your Facebook privacy is to determine who, by default, can see all the posts you make. You can do this in a positive fashion, by telling Facebook precisely who can view your new posts. You can also take a more negative (or defensive) approach, by telling Facebook who *can't* see your status updates.

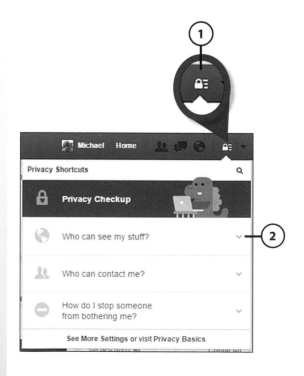

1. Click the Privacy Shortcuts button on the Facebook toolbar to display the pull-down menu.

2. Click the down arrow next to Who Can See My Stuff? to expand the menu.

3. Go to the Who Can See My Future Posts? section, click the down arrow, and select one of the resulting options.

4. Click Public to let anyone on Facebook see your posts.

5. Click Friends to restrict viewing to only people on your Facebook friends list.

6. Click Only Me to keep your posts totally private—that is, to keep anyone from seeing them.

7. Click More Options to further expand the menu.

8. Click Friends Except Acquaintances to restrict viewing to people on your Facebook friends list, minus those you've classified as "acquaintances" to see fewer of their posts.

9. Click Custom to create a custom list of people who can or can't see your posts. The Custom Privacy panel displays.

10. In the Share This With box, enter the names of friends or friends list you want to share with.

11. To share with friends of people you tag in your posts or photos, check the Friends of Tagged option.

12. To *not* share your posts with a given friend or friends list, enter that name into the Don't Share This With box.

13. Click the Save Changes button.

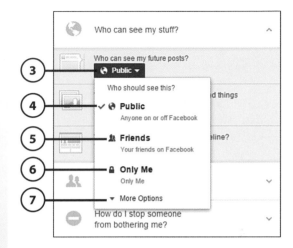

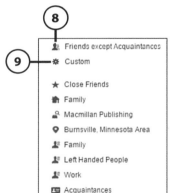

Select Who Can See (or Not See) Individual Posts

Even after you set these global posting privacy settings, you can change the privacy setting for any individual post you make. That is, any given post can be sent to a specific list of people that overrides the global settings you made previously.

For example, you might have set your global privacy settings so that your friends can see your posts. But if you have a new post that you only want your immediate family to see, you can configure that single post to go only to your family members, not to everyone else on your friends list.

New Default

When you change the privacy setting for an individual post, that setting becomes the new default for all future posts.

1. Go to your Facebook Home page, start a new status update as you normally would, then click the Post Privacy Setting button and select one of the following options.

2. Click Public to make this post visible to any Facebook user.

3. Click Friends to make this post visible to only those on your friends list.

4. Click Only Me to keep your posts totally private—that is, to keep anyone from seeing them.

5. Click More Options to further expand the menu.

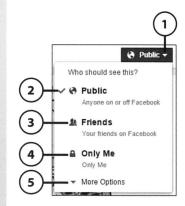

6. Click Friends Except Acquaintances to restrict viewing to people on your Facebook friends list, minus those you've classified as "acquaintances."

7. Click Custom to display the Custom Privacy panel and then specify the people who can see this post.

8. Select the necessary options to make this post visible or to hide it from specific people or lists.

9. Click the Save Changes button.

Friends except Acquaintances
Custom

Close Friends
Family
Macmillan Publishing
Burnsville, Minnesota Area
Family
Left Handed People

Custom Privacy

+ **Share with**

These people or lists   Friends ×

Friends of tagged   ✓

Note: Anyone tagged can also see this post.

× **Don't share with**

These people or lists

Cancel   Save Changes

Limiting Contact from Other Members

Are you getting private messages or friend requests from people you don't know? It's time to reconfigure your privacy settings to limit contact from complete strangers.

Control Who Can Contact You

By default, just about anybody who Facebook thinks you might know can send you private messages. If you'd rather not be contacted by complete strangers, you can tell Facebook to only let your friends send you messages.

1. From the Facebook toolbar, click the Privacy Shortcuts button to display the drop-down menu.

2. Click the down arrow next to Who Can Contact Me? to expand this section.

3. Basic Filtering is selected by default. Select Strict Filtering to see private messages only from people on your friends list.

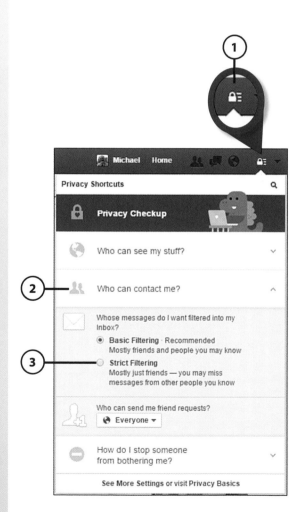

Control Who Can Send You Friend Requests

You can also limit who on Facebook can request to be your friend. By default, anyone on Facebook can friend you; however, you might not want to see friend requests from people you don't know.

1. From the Facebook toolbar, click the Privacy Shortcuts button to display the drop-down menu.

2. Click the down arrow next to Who Can Contact Me? to expand this section.

3. Go to the Who Can Send Me Friend Requests? section and click the Privacy button. (By default, the button says "Everyone.")

4. Click Friends of Friends to limit friend requests to people who know the people you know—people who are friends with your Facebook friends. (If you choose this option, however, any long-lost friends who don't know your other friends won't be able to contact you.)

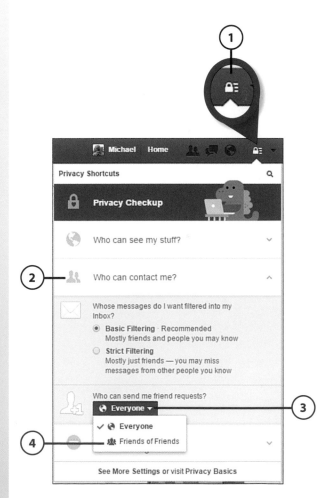

Controlling Tagging

Facebook likes to connect people with each other. This is often done via *tagging*, where one user can tag ("who are you with?") another user in a status update or photo without asking the other person. When you're tagged, you're connected to that post or photo, whether you want to be or not—which can be an invasion of your privacy.

Restrict Who Sees Tag Suggestions in Photos That Look Like You

One of the ways that Facebook encourages tagging is by suggesting people to tag when someone posts a photo. Facebook does this via facial recognition technology; it compares a given photo with the millions of other photos uploaded to its site, and tries to match a new face with one it already knows.

So if someone uploads a picture of someone that looks like you, Facebook suggests that you be tagged in that photo. That's fine, unless that's not really you—or if the photo is one you'd rather not be associated with. Fortunately, you can turn off these photo tag suggestions.

It's Not All Good

You Can Still Be Tagged

Just because you turn off Facebook's ability to suggest your name when someone uploads a photo, that doesn't mean you can't be tagged in that photo. The person who uploaded the photo can still manually tag you, even if your name isn't automatically suggested.

1. From the Facebook toolbar, click the down arrow button to display the menu of options.

2. Click Settings to display the Account Settings page.

3. Click Timeline and Tagging in the left-hand column to display the Timeline and Tagging Settings page.

4. Go to the How Can I Manage Tags People Add and Tagging Suggestions? section.

5. Go to the Who Sees Tag Suggestions When Photos That Look Like You Are Uploaded? option and click Edit.

6. Click the Privacy button to see the list of options.

7. By default, Friends is selected, which means that all of your friends will see your name in their tag suggestions. Click No One to keep your name from appearing as a tag suggestion for anyone, including your friends.

Limit Who Can See Posts You're Tagged In

As noted, there's nothing to stop friends from manually tagging you in the posts they make and the photos they upload. What you can do, however, is keep anyone else from seeing those tags—in effect, hiding your name when tagged.

1. From the Facebook toolbar, click the down arrow button to display the menu of options.

2. Click Settings to display the Account Settings page.

3. Click Timeline and Tagging in the left-hand column to display the Timeline and Tagging Settings page.

4. Go to the Who Can See Things on My Timeline? section.

5. Go to the Who Can See Posts You've Been Tagged In On Your Timeline? option and click Edit.

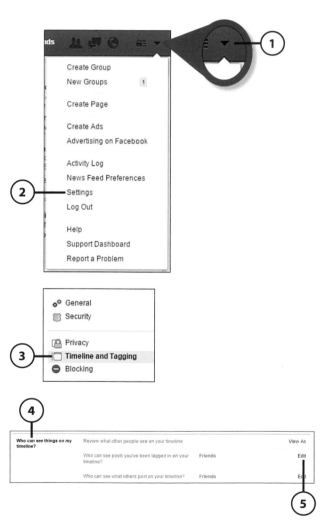

6. Click the Privacy button to display the list of options.

7. Click Friends to limit your exposure to only people on your friends list.

8. Click Only Me to hide your name from everyone on Facebook.

Approve Tags People Add to Your Posts

Here's a real invasion of your privacy. You post a picture to Facebook, and someone tags himself in your photo—even if it's not really a picture of him! Fortunately, Facebook gives you the option of reviewing all tags that people add to the posts you make and the photos you upload—so you can restrict who "associates" with you online.

1. From the Facebook toolbar, click the down arrow button to display the menu of options.

2. Click Settings to display the Account Settings page.

3. Click Timeline and Tagging in the left-hand column to display the Timeline and Tagging Settings page.

4. Go to the How Can I Manage Tags People Add and Tagging Suggestions? section.

5. Go to the Review Tags People Add to Your Own Posts Before the Tags Appear on Facebook? option and click Edit.

6. Click the Privacy button to see the list of options.

7. Click Enabled. You are notified whenever someone tries to add his or her tag to one of your posts or photos, and you have the option of approving or rejecting that tag.

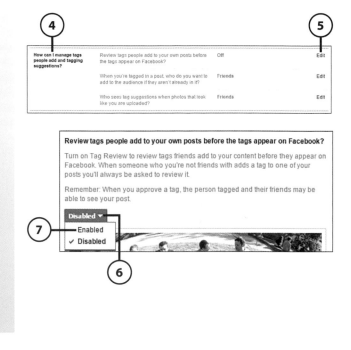

Managing Who Sees What on Your Timeline

Another place that Facebook displays personal information is on your Timeline, which is your profile page on Facebook. Fortunately, you can limit who can see specific information there—and hide entire sections if you like.

Control Who Sees Specific Information

Any given section in your Timeline has its own privacy settings. That is, you can configure different parts of your Timeline to be visible to different groups of people. For example, you can configure your Timeline so that everyone on Facebook can see your About section, but limit viewing of your Photos section to only people on your friends list.

1. Click your name on the toolbar to display your Timeline page.

2. Click the Update Info button.

3. In the left column, select the type of information you want to configure.

4. Mouse over the individual item you want to change and then click Edit.

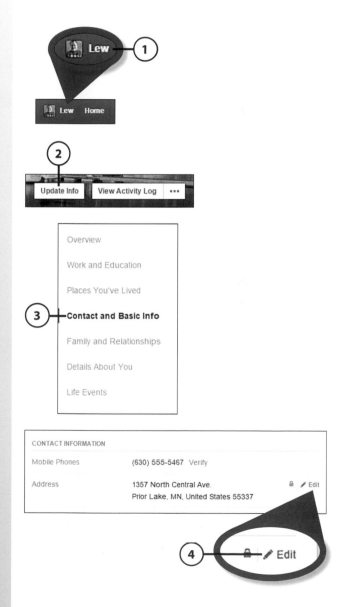

5. Click the Privacy button for the piece of information you want to configure.

6. Select who can see this information: Public (everyone on Facebook), Friends (people on your friends list), Friends Except Acquaintances, Only Me (no one can see it), Custom, or one of your customized friends lists.

7. Click the Save Changes button.

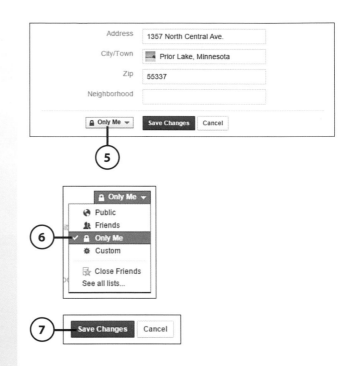

Hide Sections of Your Timeline

In addition to setting privacy options for individual pieces of information, you can also choose to hide entire sections of your Timeline. For example, if you don't want anyone to see the Places you've been or Music you've listened to, you can hide those sections.

1. Click your name on the toolbar to display your Timeline page.

2. Click the About tab.

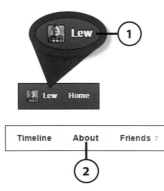

3. Scroll down to the section you want to hide and click the Manage (pencil) button for that section.

4. Click Hide Section.

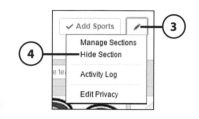

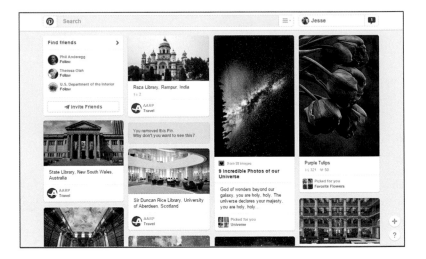

- → Getting to Know Pinterest
- → Viewing and Repinning Pins
- → Pinning on Pinterest
- → Creating New Pinterest Boards

9

Pinning and Repinning on Pinterest

Pinterest (www.pinterest.com) is a newer social network with particular appeal to middle-aged and older women—although there are a growing number of male users, too.

Getting to Know Pinterest

Unlike Facebook, which lets you post text-based status updates, Pinterest is all about images. The site consists of a collection of boards, like virtual corkboards, that people use to share pictures they find interesting. Users *pin* photos and other images to their personal boards, and then they share their pins with online friends.

Pins on Pinterest are more than just pretty pictures, however. When you click a pin, it links back to the web page for that particular image. This way you can read more information about an image—or get a detailed recipe or set of instructions for a home improvement project.

You can pin images of anything—clothing, furniture, recipes, do-it-yourself (DIY) projects, and the like. Your Pinterest friends can then *repin* your images to their own boards—and on and on.

A Pinterest board becomes a place where you can create and share collections of those things you like or find interesting. You can have as many boards as you like, organized by category or topic.

Friends who follow you see the images you pin, and you see the ones they pin. You can also *like* other people's pins and repin their items to your boards, thus repeating the original pin. It's a visual way to share things you like online.

Joining and Logging In to Pinterest

Joining Pinterest is free; in fact, you can sign up using your Facebook username and password (or with your email address, of course).

1. From your web browser, go to **www.pinterest.com**.

2. To create a new account, click the Sign Up button and follow the onscreen instructions.

3. To sign in to Pinterest with your Facebook account, click the Continue with Facebook button. If you're currently logged into Facebook, you'll be taken directly to Pinterest; if not, you'll be prompted to enter your Facebook user name (email address) and password. Follow the onscreen instructions from there.

4. To sign in to an existing Pinterest account, enter your email address and password, and then click the Log In button.

Navigating the Pinterest Site

Pinterest is a relatively easy website to get around. After you've logged on, it's a simple matter of displaying and viewing pins and boards.

1. When you first log in to Pinterest, you see the Home page. Pins from boards and users you follow are listed here; scroll down to view older pins.

2. To search for specific pins or users, enter your query into the Search box at the top of the page.

3. Click your name to view your own boards and pins.

4. Click the Notifications button to view notifications from Pinterest and information about which of your pins have been repinned.

5. Click the Pinterest button to return to the home page from any other page of the site.

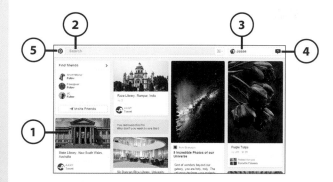

Viewing and Repinning Pins

All items pinned on Pinterest have the same overall format. You can view more information about any pin, as well as the person who pinned it. You can also "repin" a pin to one of your own boards.

View a Pin

Pins from people and boards you follow are displayed in the visual feed
on your Pinterest home page.

1. Mouse over the image to display
   the action buttons.

2. Click the heart button to like
   this pin.

3. Click the user's name/board
   name to display all the pins in
   this particular board.

4. Click the pinned image to view
   the pin's details page.

5. Click the Visit Site button (or just
   click the image itself) to view
   the website where the image
   was originally found.

6. Click the board's name to view
   all the pins in this particular
   board.

7. To comment on this pin,
   enter your text into the Add a
   Comment box.

8. To follow all the pins from this
   user, click the Follow button
   next to the user's name.

9. Scroll further down to view pins
   similar to this one.

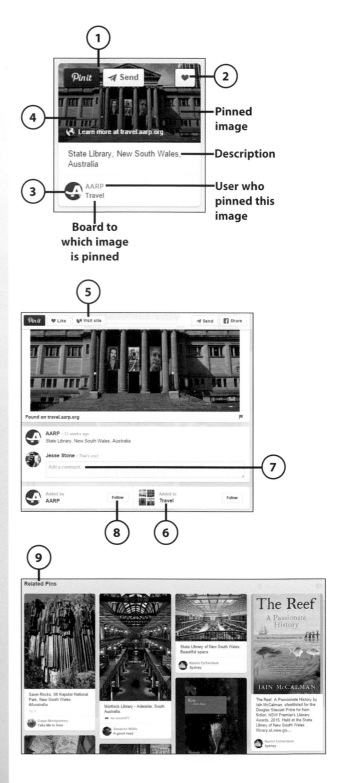

Repin a Pin

Some people say that Pinterest is a little like a refrigerator covered with magnets holding up tons of photos and drawings. You can find lots of interesting items pinned from other users—and then "repin" them to your own personal boards.

1. Mouse over the item you want to repin and click the Pin It button. The Pick a Board panel displays.

2. Accept the existing description or click the description to enter your own.

3. Click the board to which you want to pin this item. The item is now pinned to that board.

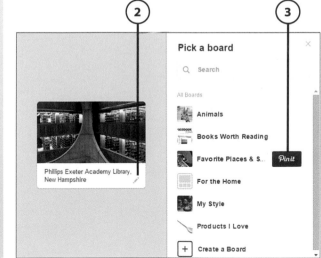

Pinning on Pinterest

In addition to repinning items you find on the Pinterest site, you can also pin images you find on the web—or those stored on your own computer.

Pin an Item from a Web Page

To pin an image you find on a web page, all you need is that page's web address.

1. From any Pinterest page, click the + button in the lower right corner.

2. Click Pin from a Website to display the Pin from a Website panel.

3. Enter the web address (URL) of the page you want to pin into the bottom text box.

4. Click the Next button.

5. Pinterest now displays all images found on the selected web page. Mouse over the image you want to pin and click the Pin It button to open the Pick a Board panel.

Not Always Welcome

Some websites don't want people to pin their images, so they code their pages to prohibit pinning. If you try to pin from one of these pages, you get a message that no pinnable images have been found. If you happen to pin an image that some entity owns and doesn't want you to pin, they can ask Pinterest to take down the pin. (Legally, Pinterest says it's not responsible for any copyright claims for items pinned to its site.)

6. Enter a short (500 characters or less) text description of or comment on this image into the Add a Description box.

7. Click the board to which you want to pin this image, or click Create a Board to pin the image to a new board. The image is now pinned to that board.

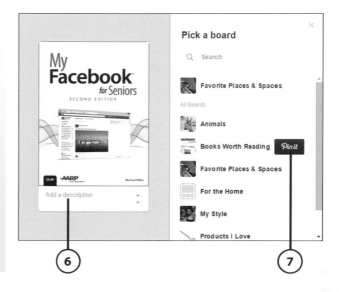

⑥   ⑦

>>>Go Further

PIN IT FROM YOUR BROWSER

It's even easier to pin an image from a web page if you install Pinterest's Browser Button in your web browser. To do this, click the + button and select Save Ideas Faster with the Pin It button. Follow the onscreen instructions to install the Pin It button in your browser's toolbar.

When you next visit a web page that you'd like to pin from, click the Pin It button in your browser. You'll see images from this web page; click the Pin It button for the image you want to pin and proceed from there.

Upload a Pin from Your Computer

You can also create new pins from images stored on your computer.

1. From any Pinterest page, click the + button in the lower right corner.

2. Click Upload a Pin to display the Upload a Pin panel.

3. Click the Choose Image button to display the Open window.

4. Navigate to and select the image file you want to upload.

5. Click the Open button.

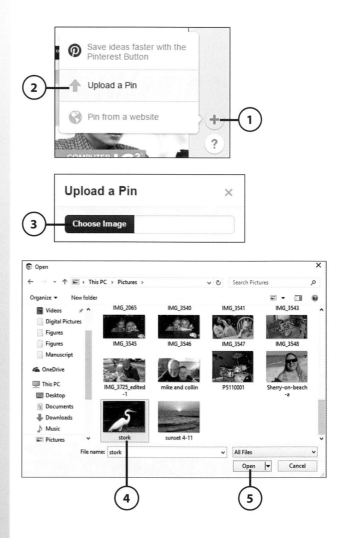

6. The image is now uploaded, and Pinterest displays the Pick a Board panel. Enter a description for this item into the Add a Description box.

7. Click the board to which you want to pin this image, or click Create a Board to pin the image to a new board. The image is now pinned to that board.

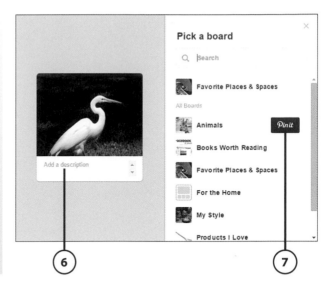

Creating New Pinterest Boards

Pinterest lets you create any number of boards, each dedicated to specific topics. If you're into quilting, you can create a Quilting board; if you're into radio-controlled airplanes, you can create an RC Airplanes board with pictures of your favorite craft.

Create a Board

When you first join Pinterest, you need to create boards to match your personal tastes. You can create new boards at any time—and as many as you like.

1. Click your name in the Pinterest toolbar to display all your boards.

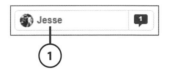

2. Click the Create a Board tile to display the Create a Board panel.

3. Enter the name for this board into the Name box.

4. Enter a short description of this board into the Description box.

5. Pull down the Category list and select a general category for this board.

6. Ignore the Map, Keep It Secret, Collaborators, and Members Can Invite Others options.

7. Click the Create Board button.

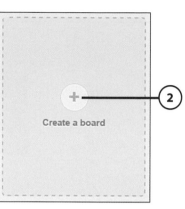

View Your Boards and Pins

You can view all your boards and pins from your personal page on Pinterest.

1. Click your name in the Pinterest toolbar to display all your boards.

2. To display your pins, click the Pins tab.

3. To display those pins you've liked, click the Like tab.

4. To display people following your pins, click the Followers tab.

5. To display users and boards that you are following, click the Following tab.

6. To view the items pinned to a given board, click that board.

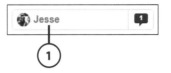

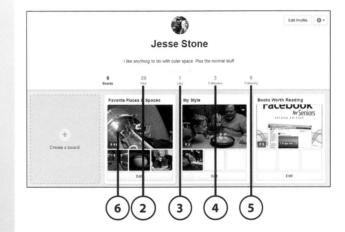

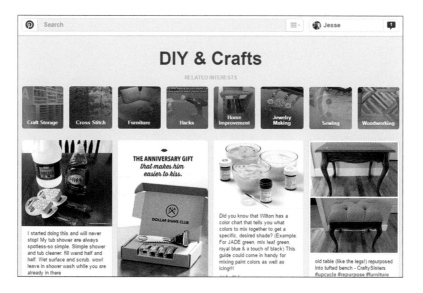

In this chapter, you learn how to find pins, boards, and people on Pinterest.

→ Browsing and Searching for Pins
→ Searching for People and Boards

Finding Other Users and Boards to Follow on Pinterest

How do you find items to repin on Pinterest? It's a matter of searching or browsing for specific types of items—and for other pinners to follow.

Browsing and Searching for Pins

With more than 50 billion pins in more than one billion boards, there's a lot of interesting content to find on Pinterest. How do you sort through all those pins to find the ones you want to repin?

Browse via Category

Pinterest organizes its pins into a relative handful of major categories. You can browse through the categories to find the most popular pins of a given type.

1. Click the Categories (three-line) button in the Pinterest toolbar to display available categories.

2. Click a category to see pins within that category.

3. Most categories are divided into further categories, listed at the top of the category page. Click a subcategory to view pins within that subcategory.

4. To repin a pin, mouse over that pin and click the Pin It button.

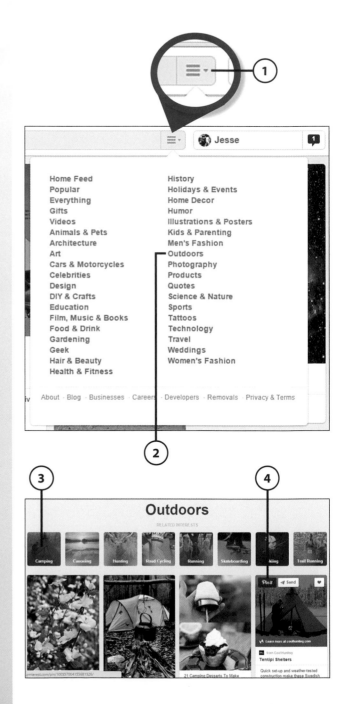

Search by Keyword

You can also search for pins of a certain type by entering one or more keywords that describe what you're looking for.

1. Click within the Search box in the toolbar and enter one or more keywords.

2. As you type, Pinterest displays suggested searches. If one of these is what you're looking for, click it.

3. Otherwise, continue entering your query then press Enter.

4. Pinterest now displays pins that match your query. You can fine-tune your search by selecting one of the filters displayed at the top of the search results page.

5. To repin a pin, mouse over that pin and click the Pin It button.

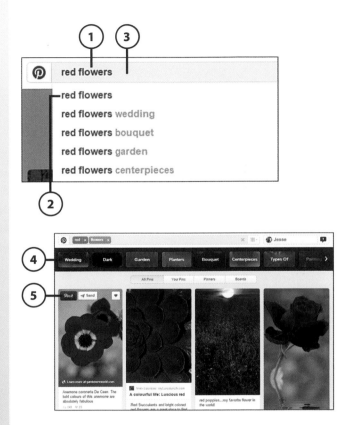

Searching for People and Boards

Pinterest also lets you search for boards about a given topic, which you can then follow. You can also search for individual users—and follow them, too. (Pins from any board or user you follow appear in the feed on your Pinterest home page.)

Find and Follow Interesting Boards

Just as you can search for individual pins, you can also search for boards full of pins in which you might be interested.

1. Click within the Search box in the toolbar and enter one or more keywords that describe what you're looking for.

2. As you type, Pinterest displays suggested searches. If one of these is what you're looking for, click it.

3. Otherwise, continue entering your query then press Enter.

4. Pinterest now displays pins that match your query. Click the Boards button to instead display matching boards.

5. Click a board to view all the pins pinned to that board.

6. Click the Follow button to follow pins made to that board.

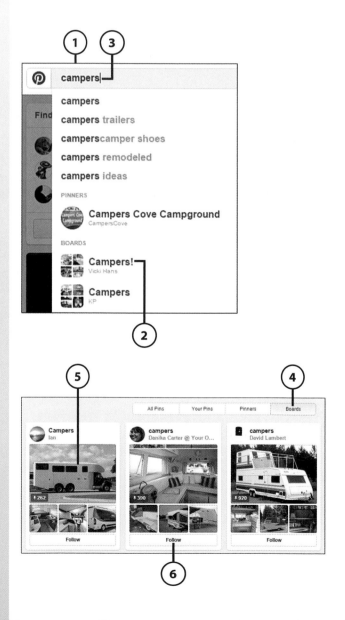

Find Other Users to Follow

While you can search for individual users by name or by keyword from the Pinterest Search box, a better approach is to find a pin you like and then click through to learn more about the person who pinned that item. You can then opt to follow that person or specific boards created by that person. (Following a person means that all that person's new pins display on your Pinterest home page.)

1. When you find a pin you like, click the name of the person who pinned it to see the board for that pin.

2. On the board page, click the person's name to see all of their boards.

3. Click the Follow button to follow all of this person's pins.

4. Alternatively, if you only want to follow pins to one of this person's boards, click the Follow button for the board you want to follow.

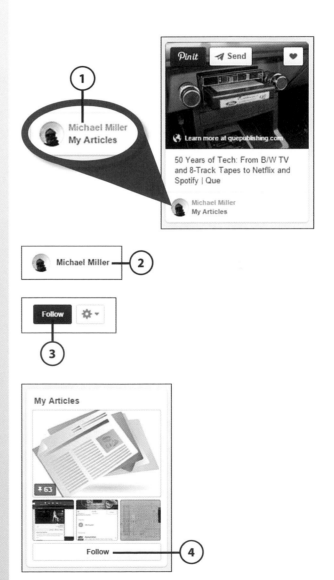

Unfollow a Board

Over time, you may find that some boards you follow aren't quite as interesting as you once thought. Fortunately, you can opt to unfollow any board at any time.

1. Click your name in the Pinterest toolbar to display your personal page.

2. Click Following to display all the people and boards you follow.

3. Click Boards to display the boards you follow.

4. Find the board you no longer want to follow, and then click the Unfollow button.

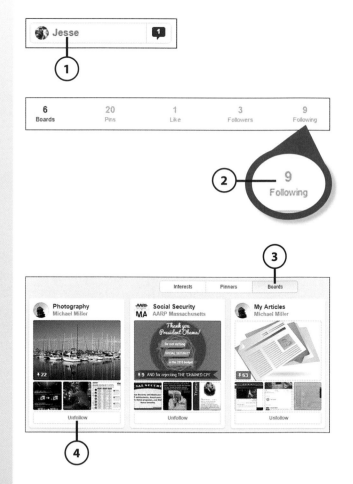

>>>*Go Further*

FOR WOMEN—AND MEN

As we've discussed, Pinterest is particularly appealing to women—more so than any other social network. Maybe it's the visual nature of Pinterest. Maybe it's because women jumped on the bandwagon first, and that encouraged even more women to join.

Whatever the reasons, Pinterest has a huge following among women of all ages. Women use Pinterest to pin the latest fashions, recipes, DIY and craft projects, you name it. My wife uses it to find recipes for the family meals. My stepdaughter uses it for gift and party ideas for her kids (my grandkids). My friend's wife actually hosts Pinterest craft nights at our church, with fun crafts found on the Pinterest site. You get the idea.

That's not to say that Pinterest is only a female thing. It's not. More and more men are joining Pinterest and pinning items of interest to them. Some of my friends have Pinterest boards for classic automobiles, baseball cards, favorite golf courses, and various other sports and hobbies (including DIY projects, of course—that topic definitely crosses genders). Personally, I've played drums for the past half century, so I have boards devoted to famous drummers, cool drum sets, and musicians in general.

In short, you can use Pinterest to follow anything in which you have an interest. It doesn't matter whether you're male or female, what age you are, or how much money you make. Pinterest is a social network for anyone and everyone.

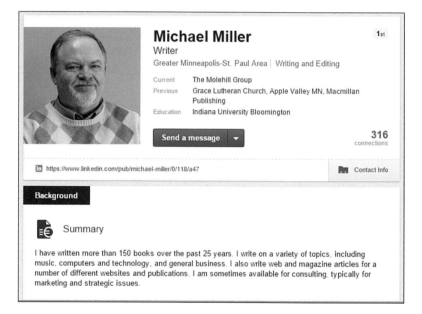

Michael Miller

1st

Writer

Greater Minneapolis-St. Paul Area | Writing and Editing

Current   The Molehill Group

Previous   Grace Lutheran Church, Apple Valley MN, Macmillan
              Publishing

Education   Indiana University Bloomington

Send a message ▼

316
connections

https://www.linkedin.com/pub/michael-miller/0/118/a47

Contact Info

Background

Summary

I have written more than 150 books over the past 25 years. I write on a variety of topics, including music, computers and technology, and general business. I also write web and magazine articles for a number of different websites and publications. I am sometimes available for consulting, typically for marketing and strategic issues.

In this chapter, you learn how to create an effective profile for professional networking on the LinkedIn social network.

→ Signing Up and Logging In
→ Creating an Effective Profile

11

Fine-Tuning Your Professional Profile on LinkedIn

LinkedIn is different from Facebook and most other social media, in that it has a distinct focus on business. Businesses use LinkedIn to find potential employees; job hunters use LinkedIn to look for potential employers; and business professionals use LinkedIn to keep in touch with others in their professions.

Even if you're not currently in the job market, LinkedIn is a great way to network with other people in your industry, and to keep tabs on what former co-workers are up to. It's very much a business networking site, using social networking functionality.

Signing Up and Logging In

Basic LinkedIn membership is free; anyone can join. LinkedIn also offers a variety of Premium memberships, from $29.99 to $79.99 per month, designed specifically for serious job hunters, business networkers, and sales professionals. For most people, however, the free membership is the way to go.

Create a New Account

When you create your LinkedIn account, you're prompted to enter some basic information, including your job status. You need to do this to create your account, but you can come back later to edit this or enter additional information.

1. In your web browser, go to **www.linkedin.com**.

2. Enter your first name and last name into the respective boxes.

3. Enter your email address into the Email Address box.

4. Enter your desired password into the Password box.

5. Click the Join Now button.

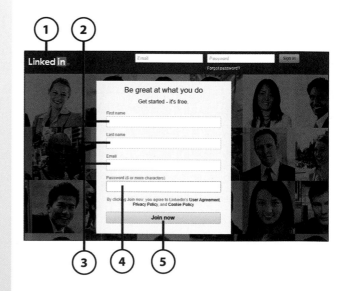

6. Pull down the Country list and select your country, if you're not in the United States.

7. Enter your ZIP code into the Zip Code box.

8. If you're a student (which you probably aren't), select Yes for the Are You a Student? option.

9. Enter your job title into the Job Title box.

10. Enter the name of your employer into the Company box.

11. When the box expands, pull down the Industry list and select the industry you're in.

12. Click the Create Your Profile button.

13. LinkedIn now asks how you want to use the site. Make a selection from the options given, or select Not Sure Yet. I'm Open!

14. You are now prompted to add your email address and import your email contacts. You can do this now or later. Click Continue to do so and then follow the onscreen instructions, or click Skip to proceed without doing this.

You're now prompted to confirm your email address. Follow the instructions to do so and proceed from there.

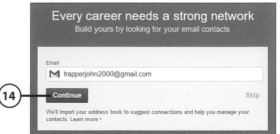

Sign In to Your Account

Once you've created your LinkedIn account, signing in is a quick and easy process.

1. In your web browser, go to **www.linkedin.com**.

2. Enter your email address into the Email Address box at the top of the page.

3. Enter your password into the Password box at the top of the page.

4. Click Sign In.

5. You now see the LinkedIn home page. Status updates from your connections are displayed on the left side of the page. Scroll down to read more.

Creating an Effective Profile

Every LinkedIn member has his or own personal profile page. This profile page is what other LinkedIn users see when they search for you on the site; it's where you make your initial impression to the people you want to make contact with—including potential employers.

Your LinkedIn profile is kind of like a mini-resume, containing important personal and professional information. It's also fully customizable; you can select which content others see.

Snapshot

Your profile page can include any or all of the following sections:

- **Snapshot.** The snapshot section is an overview of your personal information, including name, location, current title, past positions, and education. It functions as an online business card, a quick glance at your experience and qualifications. Within this section, clicking Contact Info expands the snapshot to display links to your personal website or blog, public email address, and other contact information.

- **Summary.** A paragraph or two summarizing your professional experience, specialties, and goals.

- **Experience.** A listing of your current and previous employment positions, sorted in reverse chronological order.

- **Following.** Companies that you are following—including your current employer.

- **Activity.** Displays your most recent activity on the LinkedIn site.

- **Education.** A listing of the schools you've attended, along with activities and honors, sorted in reverse chronological order.

- **Skills.** Specific professional skills you possess, as well as endorsements from other users.

You can also add sections related to your volunteering experience, certifications, interests, projects, publications, causes you support, and more.

Edit Your Snapshot

Since your profile page serves as your de facto resume on the LinkedIn site, you want to control the information you display to others. The first thing visitors to your profile page see is the snapshot section, so that's what you should edit first.

1. On the LinkedIn menu bar, click Profile and select Edit Profile. This displays your profile page.

2. The snapshot section is at the top of the page and contains any information you entered when you signed up for your LinkedIn account. To edit any existing information, mouse over that item and click the Edit (pencil) icon to display the editing pop-up.

3. Edit the desired information.

4. Click the Save button.

5. Click Add Experience to add work experience to your snapshot.

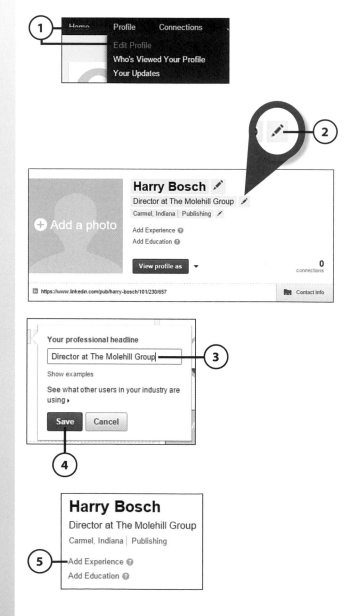

6. In the Experience section, enter the appropriate information—company name, job title, location, time period, and description.

7. Click the Save button.

8. Click Add Education to add information about your education.

9. In the Education section, enter the appropriate information—school name, dates attended, degree, field of study, and so forth.

10. Click the Save button.

Experience   + Add position

Company Name *

Title *

Location

Time Period *
Choose... ▼ Year – Choose... ▼ Year
☐ I currently work here

Description

See examples

Save   Cancel

Harry Bosch

Director at The Molehill Group

Carmel, Indiana | Publishing

Previous   Frank's BBQ

Add Education ❓

School *

Dates Attended
▼ – ▼ Or expected graduation year

Degree

Field of Study

Grade

Activities and Societies

Examples: Alpha Phi Omega, Chamber Chorale, Debate Team

Description

See examples

Save   Cancel

11. Click Contact Info to expand the snapshot panel and add/edit your contact information.

12. Mouse over the contact info you want to add or edit—email address, phone number, street address, instant messaging (IM) account, Twitter account, and so forth—then click the Edit (pencil) icon to display the editing pop-up.

13. Enter or edit the necessary information.

14. Click Save.

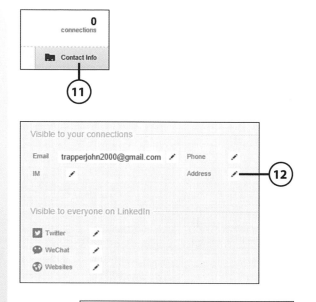

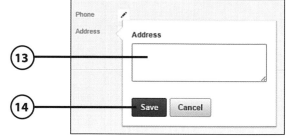

Add a Profile Picture

Profiles with pictures get much more attention than those without. You can easily add a personal picture to your LinkedIn profile.

1. On the LinkedIn menu bar, click Profile and select Edit Profile. This displays your profile page.

2. In the snapshot section, click Add a Photo to display the Edit Photo window. (If you've already added a photo, you can change it by clicking the photo.)

3. Click the Choose File button to display the Open dialog box.

4. Select the photo you wish to use.

5. Click the Open button.

6. You now see a preview of your picture in the various ways it will appear on the LinkedIn site. Use your mouse to resize or recenter the main picture.

7. Click the Save button. Your photo is now uploaded and inserted into your snapshot.

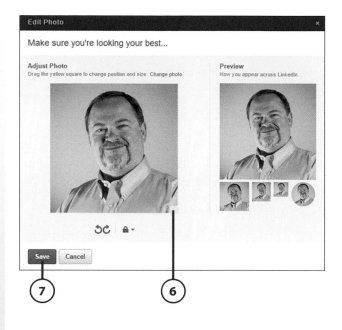

Add a Summary

The Summary section of your profile page is the place to summarize your job skills and employment history for the benefit of future employers. The Summary section doesn't appear by default, but you can add it at any time.

1. On the LinkedIn menu bar, click Profile and select Edit Profile. This displays your profile page.

2. In the Add a Section to Your Profile section, click Add Summary to display a new, empty Summary section. (If you don't see the Add Summary tile, click View More first.)

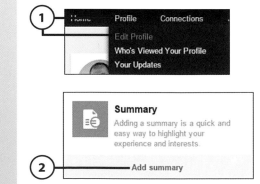

3. Enter a summary of your job skills and experience into the text box.

4. Click the Save button when done.

Write Well

Write your summary in complete sentences, using proper grammar and punctuation. Appearances matter to future employers!

Add More Sections to Your Profile

LinkedIn lets you embed additional features in your profile page by adding other sections to the page. You can choose to add sections for Certifications, Courses, Honors & Awards, Languages, Organizations, Projects, Patents, Publications, Test Scores, Volunteering Experience, and more.

1. On the LinkedIn menu bar, click Profile and select Edit Profile. This displays your profile page.

2. In the Add a Section to Your Profile section, click View More to expand the options.

3. Click the type of section you
    want to add; LinkedIn now
    displays the new, empty section.

4. Enter the requested information
    for that section.

5. Click the Save button.

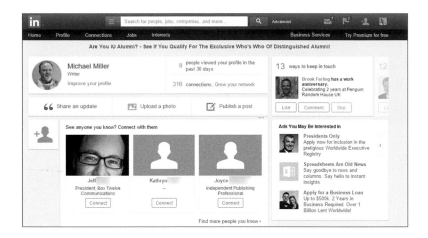

In this chapter, you discover how to connect with businesses and other professionals on the LinkedIn social network.

→ Finding New Connections
→ Sending and Receiving Messages
→ Participating in Groups

12

Connecting with People and Businesses on LinkedIn

LinkedIn, like all social media, is all about connecting. In LinkedIn's case, that means business connections—connecting with current and former co-workers, as well as others in your profession.

Business professionals use LinkedIn to expand their list of business contacts, to keep in touch with colleagues, and to keep abreast of developments in their profession. Contacts made on LinkedIn can be used for a number of different purposes, such as finding employment, making a sale, or exploring business opportunities. You can also use LinkedIn to gain an introduction to a specific individual you'd like to know, via connections with mutual contacts.

Finding New Connections

LinkedIn's equivalent of Facebook friends are called *connections*. These are business or professional contacts whom you know and trust. Anyone on the LinkedIn site can become a connection; you can also invite people who are not yet LinkedIn members to join your connections list. As with Facebook friends, people on LinkedIn have to accept your invitation before they become connections.

To establish new connections, you can search for current LinkedIn members in your email contacts list, or invite other email contacts to join LinkedIn. In addition, you can search LinkedIn for members who've gone to the same schools or worked for the same employers that you have.

Search Your Email Contacts

The first way to find new connections on LinkedIn is to let the site search your email contacts list for people who are also LinkedIn members.

1. From the LinkedIn menu bar, click Connections and then select Add Connections to display the See Who You Already Know on LinkedIn page.

2. Click the button for the email service or software you use (Gmail, Yahoo! Mail, and so on).

3. Enter your email address (and if necessary) password.

4. Click the Continue button.

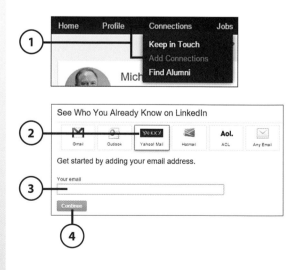

5. If prompted to sign in to your email account, do so.

6. When LinkedIn displays how it would like to use your email information, click the Agree or Yes button.

7. LinkedIn now displays all the people in your email contacts list who are also LinkedIn members. Check the names of those people you'd like to add to your LinkedIn connections list, or uncheck those names you don't want to add.

8. Click the Add Connections button (or, if there isn't anyone to add, click Skip This Step).

9. LinkedIn now recommends that you invite other email contacts to join LinkedIn. Check the names of those people you'd like to invite.

10. Click the Add to Network button.

Invitations

The people you've selected will receive invitations to become connections. If they accept your invitation, you are added to each other's connections list.

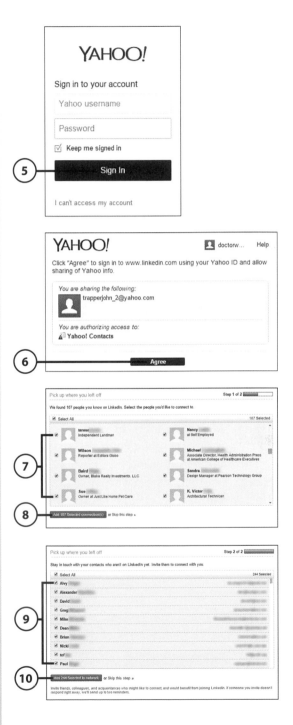

Find Former Co-Workers and Classmates

Another good source of connections are the companies you've worked for and the schools you've attended. LinkedIn helps you find other people who've shared the same employers and schools, and add them to your connections list.

1. From the LinkedIn menu bar, click Advanced next to the Search box to display the Advanced People Search panel.

2. In the Relationship section, check how close a relationship you want to search for—1st Connections (people you know directly), 2nd Connections (people who know the people you know), and so forth.

3. To search for people still employed at a given company, click Current Company, click Add, and then enter the name of the company.

4. To search for people who were previously employed at a given company, click Past Company, click Add, and then enter the name of the company.

5. To search for people who went to the same school as you, click School, click Add, and then enter the name of the school.

6. Click the Search button. LinkedIn now displays people who match your search criteria.

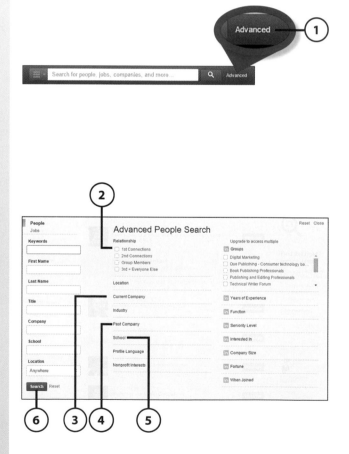

7. Those with the closest connections to you are displayed first in the list. Click the Connect button for any person to whom you'd like to establish a connection.

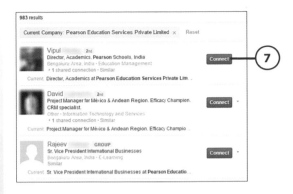

Distant Connections

LinkedIn hides the names of people who have no shared connections with you. To contact one of these people, whomever they may be, you need to upgrade to a Premium membership.

Sending and Receiving Messages

LinkedIn offers its own internal email system. This system enables you to send and receive messages to and from people you are connected to.

Read and Reply to Messages

LinkedIn's private email system is very similar to every other email system you've used, except that it works only on and within the LinkedIn site.

1. From the LinkedIn menu bar, click the Messages (envelope) icon to display your email Inbox. (If you have unread messages in your Inbox, the Messages item on the menu bar will show a number beside the Inbox text, indicating the number of unread messages waiting.)

2. You now see the latest messages you've received; unread messages are in bold and blue. To read a message, click the message header.

3. To delete a message, click the Trash icon.

4. To reply to a message, click the Reply icon. This displays the reply form, with the original message "quoted" in the text box.

5. Type your reply into the text box.

6. Click the Send Message button.

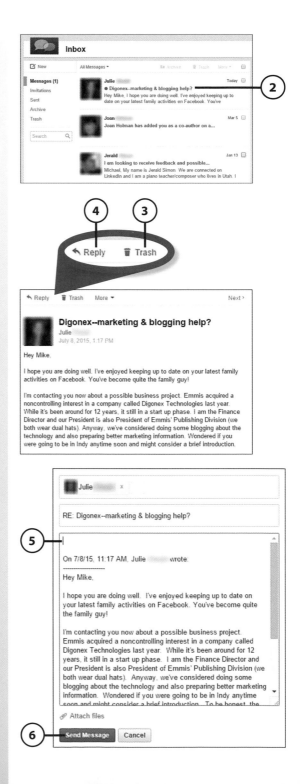

Compose a New Message

It is equally easy to send a new message to any of your LinkedIn connections.

1. From the LinkedIn menu bar, mouse over the Messages (envelope) icon and then click the New icon (or, from the Inbox page, click the New icon). This displays a new message page.

2. Enter the recipient's name or email address into the To box.

3. As you type, matching connections are displayed; click the name of the person you want to email.

4. Type the subject of the message into the Subject box.

5. Type your message into the large text box.

6. Click the Send Message button.

Post a Status Update

Like Facebook, LinkedIn enables users to post short status updates that are then displayed in their connections' home pages. (You can also publish longer "posts," but most people use the updates function.) Unlike Facebook, these status updates are not the main focus of the site; LinkedIn is still about personal connections and messages.

That said, you can let your network of connections know about important professional events in your life, by posting status updates of this nature. Likewise, your home page features status updates from your connections.

1. On the LinkedIn home page, click Share an Update. This expands the section to display a text box.

2. Click within the text box and type the text of your update.

3. To add a picture to this update, click the Upload a Photo icon and select the picture you want.

4. Click the Share With list and select how you want to share this update: Public, Just Your Connections, or Public + Twitter.

5. Click the Share button to post this update.

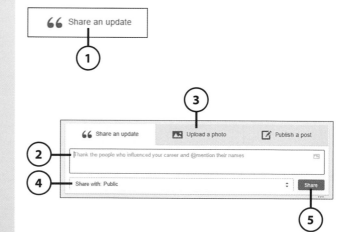

Participating in Groups

Another interesting feature of LinkedIn is its many topic-specific groups. These groups enable professionals to connect with one another regarding specific topics of mutual interest. You can join industry groups, professional groups (such as marketing or advertising groups), alumni groups, and more.

Find and Join a Group

Most LinkedIn groups are public groups, which means anyone can join. Some groups are private, which require the approval of group administrators before an application is accepted.

1. From the LinkedIn menu bar, click Interests and then select Groups. This displays the Your Groups page, with the groups you've previously joined displayed at the top.

2. Click the Find a Group button to display the Find a Group panel.

3. Enter one or more descriptive keywords into the search box.

4. Click the Search button. LinkedIn now displays groups that match your query.

5. To view a group, click the group's name.

6. To join a group, click the Join button. (Some groups only let you join from the group page; click the View button and then join from there.)

Interact with Group Members

Once you've joined a group, you can visit that group's page to interact with other group members.

1. From the LinkedIn menu bar, click Interests and then select Groups. This displays the Your Groups page, with the groups you've previously joined displayed at the top.

2. Click a group's name to open that group's page.

3. To read and comment on group discussions, click the Discussions tab.

4. To comment on an ongoing discussion, enter your comments into the Add a Comment box.

5. To start a new discussion, go to the Start a Discussion with Your Group section and enter a topic into the Enter a Discussion Title box.

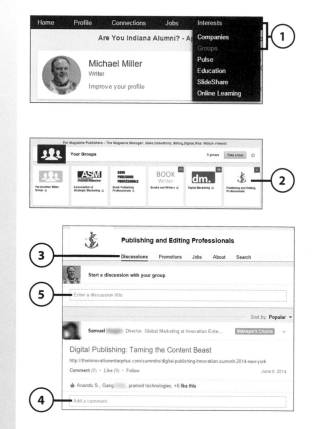

>>>*Go Further*

LOOKING FOR A JOB

Many job seekers today use social networking as a key tool in their hunt for employment. This is important for job seekers of all ages, from recent college grads to older, more experienced members of the workforce.

Employers, too, reference social networking sites when they have positions to fill, and when they're checking the qualifications of job applicants. While the full impact of social networking on hiring decisions is difficult to ascertain, recruiting site Jobvite found that, in 2014, 94 percent of recruiters used LinkedIn to find qualified job candidates—more than any other social networking site.

The most direct way to find potential employment on LinkedIn is to search the LinkedIn Jobs database. LinkedIn Jobs features thousands of job listings, organized by industry category; you can search the database by industry, company, title, experience level, date posted, and location.

LinkedIn's — Jobs page

You access LinkedIn Jobs by clicking Jobs on the LinkedIn menu bar. On the next page, enter the appropriate keywords into the search box, and then click the Search button. You can also perform more targeted searches by clicking the Advanced Search link to use the Advanced Search page.

A typical LinkedIn job listing includes a brief summary of the job (type, experience desired, functions, industry, and date posted), along with a full job description, skill requirements, and company description. Click the Apply on Company Website button to submit an application.

>>>Go Further

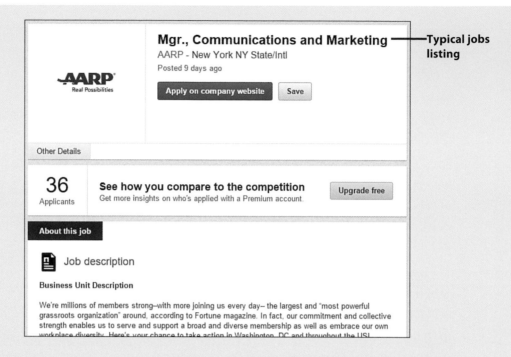

Typical jobs listing

In addition, you can use your LinkedIn connections to help you find a new position. It's possible that you may have connections—or connections of connections—within the companies for which you'd like to work. You should leverage these connections at a potential employer to learn more about the company, its culture, and its people, and to establish "inside" contacts within the company.

Tweeting and Retweeting on Twitter

Twitter is different from Facebook in that it's not a social network, but rather a microblogging service. That means it's like a Facebook but without the picture sharing and groups and such; the focus is on short (140-character) messages called *tweets*, which are shared with a user's followers.

As such, Twitter is immensely popular with younger users, but less so among older users, who value the more social nature of Facebook and Pinterest. While there aren't a whole lot of people 50+ who actively tweet, you might still want to join Twitter to follow the postings of your 20- and 30-something family members. In addition, you can use Twitter to follow breaking news, your favorite celebrities, and local organizations and events.

Signing Up and Signing On

Like most other social media, Twitter is free. If you want to follow other users' tweets, as well as tweet yourself, you need to create an account.

Create an Account

You access Twitter—and create your new account—from Twitter's home page on the web.

1. In your web browser, go to **www.twitter.com**.

2. Click the Sign Up button to display the Join Twitter Today page.

3. Enter your first and last name into the Full Name box.

4. Enter your email address or phone number into the Phone or Email box.

5. Enter your desired password into the Password box.

6. If you want Twitter to suggest tweets based on the websites you visit, check the Tailor Twitter Based on My Recent Website Visits option.

7. Click the Sign Up button, and follow the onscreen instructions from there.

Log On to Your Account

Once you've created your Twitter account, it's easy to sign in to it from any computer or smartphone.

1. In your web browser, go to **www.twitter.com**.

2. In the Log Into Your Account box, enter your email address, username, or phone number into the first box.

3. Enter your password into the second box.

4. To keep from being signed out (and having to sign back in again), check the Remember Me option.

5. Click the Log In button.

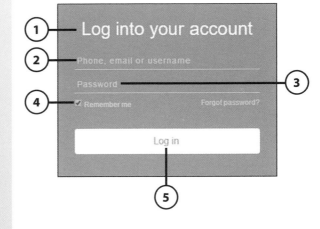

Finding Tweeters to Follow

You can follow any Twitter user. Unlike Facebook and LinkedIn, where friends and connections have to be mutually approved, you don't have to be approved to view another user's tweets. So if you want to follow Paul McCartney (@PaulMcCartney) or Fox News (@FoxNews) or just your neighbor down the street, you can do so without having to ask permission.

(The only exception to this is when a user blocks you as a follower; any user can block any other user, which helps to cut down on online stalking.)

@name

Users on Twitter are identified by a username preceded by an ampersand (@). So, for example, my username is **molehillgroup**, which translates into my Twitter "handle" of **@molehillgroup**.

Accept Twitter's Recommendations

There are several ways to find people to follow on Twitter. One approach is to accept the recommendations that Twitter makes, based on your past activities and interests.

1. On the Twitter home page, go to the Who to Follow section and click View All. Twitter now displays its recommendations.

2. To view more about a person or organization, click that entity's name.

3. To follow this person or organization, click the Follow button.

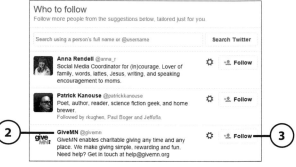

Follow Email Contacts

You can also follow people who are in your email contacts lists. Twitter will search AOL Mail, Gmail, Outlook, and Yahoo! Mail contacts.

1. On the Twitter home page, go to the Who to Follow section and click Find Friends.

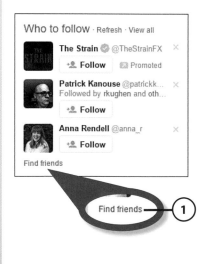

2. Click the Search Contacts button for the email service you use.

3. You may now be prompted to sign in to your email account and approve the connection. Do so and Twitter displays a list of your contacts who have Twitter accounts.

4. Check those people you'd like to follow.

5. Click the Follow *X* Selected button.

Find friends

Search your address book for friends

Choosing a service will open a window for you to log in securely and import your contacts to Twitter. We won't email anyone without your consent, but we may use contact information to improve Who To Follow suggestions.

AOL   Search contacts

M Gmail   Search contacts

Outlook   Search contacts

Y Yahoo   Search contacts ——②

You can manage the contacts you uploaded from your address book at anytime.

YAHOO!

Sign in to your account

Yahoo username

Password

☑ Keep me signed in

Sign In ——③

I can't access my account

Y Yahoo contacts Try another service

Here are 49 people for you to publicly follow. You can uncheck "Select all" or anyone you don't want to follow.

Select all 49 ✓

Dog Ear Publishing @DogEarPub
We're passionate and dedicated to helping you create, write and publish the book of your dreams!   ✓

George E Tolson @tolson_e   ✓

Chris Nelson @Factotumchris   ✓   ——④

Renee Wilmeth @feedmedrinkme
Food. Wine. Indianapolis. OG.   ✓

Julie French @JulieAnnFrench   ✓

Richard French @rickatfc   ✓

Skip this step   Follow 49 selected ——⑤

Search for People and Organizations to Follow

Twitter also lets you search for specific members and organizations to follow.

1. On the Twitter home page, go to the Who to Follow section and click View All.

2. Enter the real name or Twitter username of the person or organization you want to follow into the Search box at the top right.

3. Click the Search Twitter button. Twitter displays a list of members who match your search criteria.

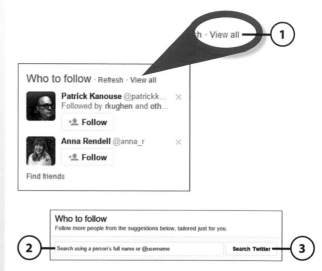

Unfollow a User

At any time, you can opt to no longer follow a particular Tweeter. This act is called *unfollowing*.

1. On the Twitter home page, in your profile box, click the Following link. Twitter now displays a list of members you are following.

2. Mouse over the Following button for the person you want to unfollow; it changes into an Unfollow button.

3. Click the Unfollow button.

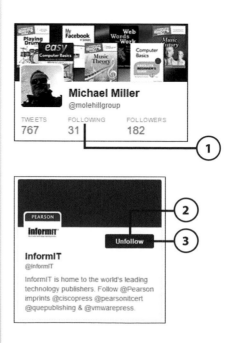

Viewing Your Twitter Feed

When you select other users to follow, you receive all their tweets on your Twitter home page. You can search for Tweeters by name or topic, or find people to follow in your email contacts lists.

View Tweets

A tweet is a text-based post to the Twitter service. Each tweet must be 140 characters or less in length. Tweets can include images, videos, and links to other web pages. They're displayed on the sender's profile page and are delivered to the sender's followers.

1. From the Twitter toolbar, click Home to display your home page.

2. Tweets are listed in reverse chronological order, with the newest tweets at the top. The name of the sender and how long ago the tweet was made are listed at the top of each tweet. Scroll down the page to view older tweets.

3. To view the profile summary for a given person, click that person's name or @name within the tweet.

4. To "like" a tweet, mouse over the tweet and click the star (Favorite) icon.

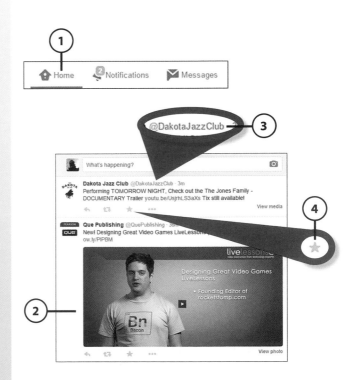

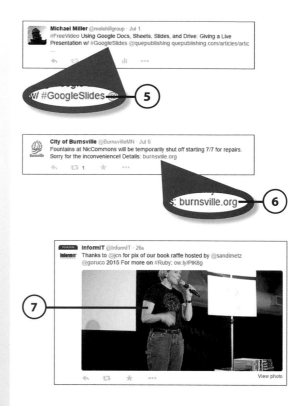

5. To view other tweets on a highlighted topic, click the hashtag (#topic) within the tweet.

6. To view a web page linked to within a tweet, click the embedded URL.

7. Photos are embedded within tweets, but at a limited height. To view the full picture, click it.

Reply to a Tweet

You can reply to any tweet you read. All you have to do is click the Reply button next to the sender's username in the original tweet. Your reply will be sent as a tweet back to the original sender.

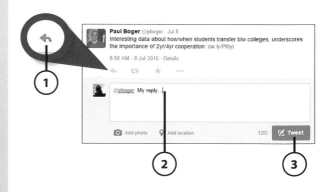

1. From the Twitter home page, click the Reply icon for the tweet to which you want to reply. This opens a reply box beneath the original tweet.

2. The sender's name appears in the reply box, preceded by the @ sign. Enter your reply (140 characters max) into the reply box.

3. Click the Tweet button to send the reply as a tweet.

Retweet a Tweet

A *retweet* (RT) is a tweet that you resend to people who are following you. This is an efficient way to obtain wide distribution for popular tweets you find in your feed.

City of Burnsville @BurnsvilleMN 3h
Seniors 62+ - join the fun at the Golden Summer Games! Includes pickleball, bean bags & more. Register by Friday. burnsville.org/recreation

1. From the Twitter home page, click the Retweet icon for the tweet to which you want to retweet. This displays the Retweet This to Your Followers? panel.

Retweet this to your followers?   ×

Add a comment...

City of Burnsville @BurnsvilleMN 3h
Seniors 62+ - join the fun at the Golden Summer Games! Includes pickleball, bean bags & more. Register by Friday. burnsville.org/recreation

Retweet

2. Add any additional comments in the Add a Comment box.

3. Click the Retweet button.

Posting Your Own Tweets

You can tweet from your computer, using your web browser to access the Twitter site. You can also tweet from your mobile phone or tablet, using Twitter's mobile app.

Post a Tweet

Because of the 140-character limitation, tweets do not have to conform to proper grammar, spelling, and sentence structure—and, in fact, seldom do. It is common to abbreviate longer words, use familiar acronyms, substitute single letters and numbers for whole words, and refrain from all punctuation. (For example, you might shorten the sentence "I'll see you on Friday" to read "C U Fri.")

1. From anywhere on the Twitter site, click the Tweet button on the toolbar. This displays the Compose New Tweet panel.

2. Type your message into the large text box. Remember that a tweet can be no more than 140 characters in length.

3. Click the Tweet button.

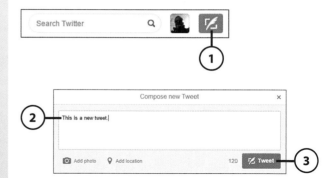

Web Links

To add a link to another website to your tweet, simply type the URL as part of your message. You may wish to use a link-shortening service, such as bit.ly (www.bit.ly), to create shorter URLs to fit within Twitter's 140-character limit.

Mention Other Users

When you mention other Twitter users in your tweets, their names become clickable by anyone viewing the tweets. Clicking a referenced name displays that user's Twitter profile summary.

1. Start a new tweet as normal.

2. Type an ampersand (@) before the user's name, like this: **@username**.

3. Click the Tweet button to post the tweet.

Use Hashtags

When you add a hash character (#) before a specific word in a tweet, that word gets referenced by Twitter as a kind of keyword, or *hashtag*, and that word becomes clickable by anyone viewing the tweet. Clicking a hashtag in a tweet displays a list of the most recent tweets that include the same hashtag.

1. Start a new tweet as normal.

2. Type a hash character or pound sign (#) before the word you want to reference, like this: **#keyword**.

3. Click the Tweet button to post the tweet.

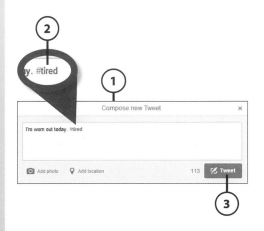

>>>Go Further
HASHTAGS

A *hashtag* is a word or phrase (with no spaces) in a tweet that is preceded by the hash or pound character, like this: **#hashtag**. Hashtags function much like keywords, by helping other users find relevant tweets when searching for a particular topic. A hashtag within a tweet is clickable; clicking a hashtag displays a list of the most recent tweets that include that word.

You can use hashtags to find tweets related to a given topic. Hashtags are particularly valuable when looking for information on a current or trending topic.

For this reason, it's common (and expected) for tweets to include one or more hashtags. The more you can use hashtags to connect to popular and trending topics, the better.

Tweet a Picture

While tweets started out as text-only posts, Twitter now lets you embed images in your tweets.

1. Start a new tweet as you normally would.

2. Click the Add Photo button to display the Open dialog box.

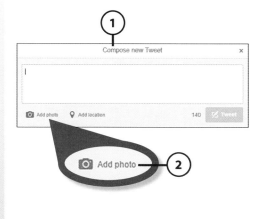

3. Select the photo you wish to use.

4. Click the Open button.

5. The attached photo now appears as a thumbnail beneath the text box. To tag a person in this photo, click Who's In This Photo?

6. Start typing the person's name. Twitter now displays users who match your search.

7. Choose someone from this list, or continue typing the person's name and press Enter.

8. Click the Tweet button to post the tweet.

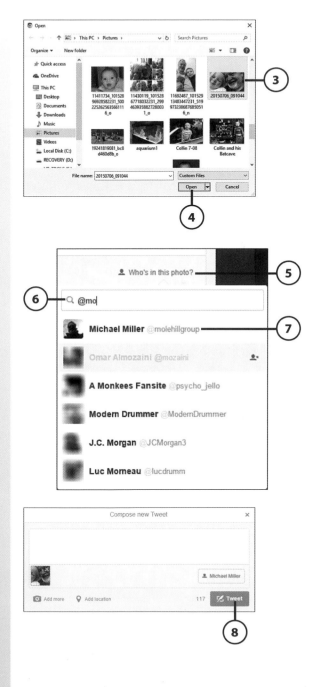

In this chapter, you learn how to use the Instagram app to shoot, share, and view digital photos and videos on your smartphone.

→ Getting Started with Instagram
→ Following Friends and Family
→ Shooting and Sharing Photos and Videos

14

Sharing Photos with Instagram

Instagram is different from other social media discussed in this book in that it's solely a mobile medium. You install the Instagram app on your smartphone or tablet and then use that app to shoot photos, share those photos with others, and browse photos shot and shared by your friends and family.

You can use Instagram purely as a photo app, as a photo sharing app, or as a viewer for the photos others share with you. You don't have to post any photos to use Instagram; in fact, many people use Instagram solely as a way to view photos shot and shared by other family members.

Getting Started with Instagram

Let's be honest; Instagram is much more popular among younger users than people our age. There are probably lots of good reasons for this, not the least of which is that people in their 20s and 30s shoot a lot more photos (especially photos of their kids) than do people in their 50s, 60s, and 70s. Instagram lets them shoot and edit their photos, all on their smartphones, and then—in the same app—share those photos with other family and friends.

Even if you don't plan on using Instagram to shoot or share photos you take, it still may be a good idea to install the Instagram app on your mobile device and sign up for a (free) Instagram account.

Download and Install the Instagram App

Instagram is both a mobile app for your smartphone or tablet and a social network. Versions of the Instagram app are available for Apple's iPhones, Android phones, and Windows Phone devices. You can download the app (for free) from Apple's App Store, the Google Play Store, or the Windows Phone Store.

Mobile Apps

The Instagram app for Android differs slightly from the one for Apple's iPhones and iPads. We use the Android app for examples here; if you're using an Apple device, your screens may look slightly different.

Sign Up for a New Account

Once you have the Instagram app installed, you launch the app by tapping its icon on your phone's home screen. The first time you launch the app, you're prompted to either sign in to an existing account or create a new one.

1. Tap the Instagram icon to launch the app.

2. Tap Sign Up. (Alternatively, you can tap Log In with Facebook to log in with your Facebook account.)

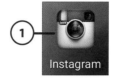

Log in with your Facebook account

3. Enter your email address, and then tap Next.

4. Enter your full name, and then tap Next.

5. Enter your desired username, and then tap Next.

6. Enter your desired password, and then tap Next.

7. You are now prompted to add a profile photo. You can import a photo from Facebook or Twitter, take a new photo, or use a photo stored in your phone's photo library. Tap the desired selection or tap Skip to not choose a photo at this point in time.

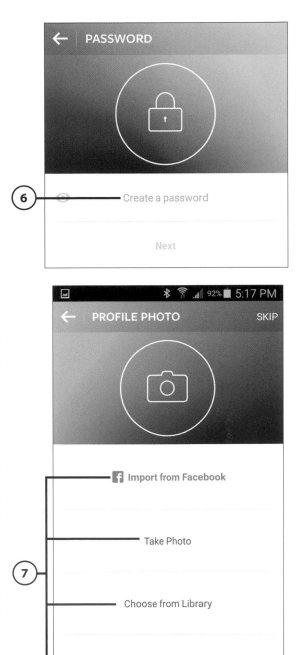

8. You are now prompted to find friends who are on Instagram. You can do this now or skip this process and do it later.

9. Instagram now prompts you to search your contacts for friends who are also on the service. You can do this now or skip this process and do it later.

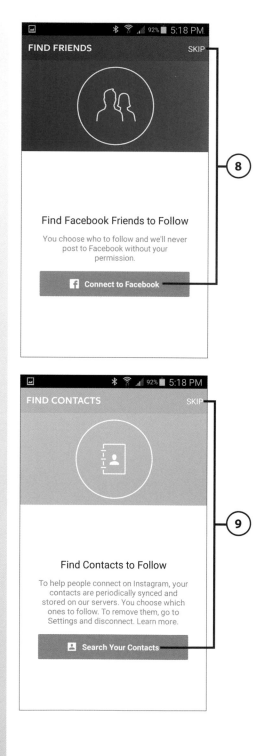

10. Now you're prompted to select topics to follow. You can do this if you want, or tap the right arrow to proceed without doing so. You're now ready to begin using Instagram.

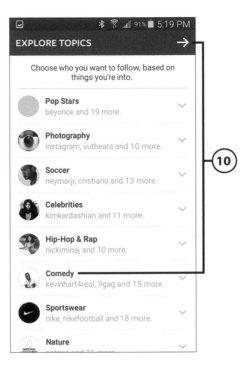

Edit Your User Profile

The next time you open the Instagram app, you're automatically logged in to your account. You can then edit the profile information that other users see.

1. From within the Instagram app, tap the Profile button to display your profile.

2. Tap Edit Your Profile to display the Edit Profile screen.

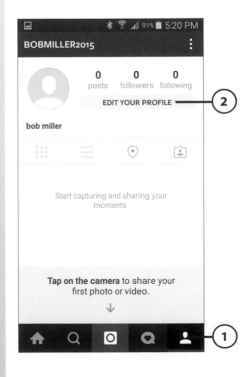

3. Tap the item you wish to edit or enter, and then enter the necessary information.

4. Tap the checkmark when done.

Link to Your Other Social Media Accounts

As part of the initial setup process, you should also link your Instagram account to your other social media. This lets you share the photos you shoot with your Facebook, Twitter, and other online friends and family.

1. From within the Instagram app, tap the Profile button to display your profile.

2. Tap the Options (three button or gear) icon to display the Options screen.

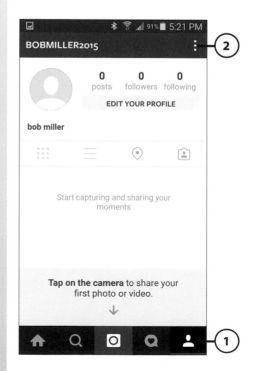

3. Scroll down to the Settings section and tap Linked Accounts to display the Linked Accounts screen.

4. Tap the social network you wish to link to—Facebook, Twitter, Foursquare, Tumblr, or Flickr, among others.

5. If prompted, enter your sign in information for this account— typically your email/username and password, and tap the checkmark when done. (If you're already logged in to the social app, you don't have to re-log in here.)

SETTINGS

③──── Linked Accounts

Push Notifications

← **LINKED ACCOUNTS**

f Facebook

④──── Twitter

Foursquare

t Tumblr

●○ Flickr

VKontakte

✕ **TWITTER** ✓

⑤ Twitter Username

Password

We never store your password.

Following Friends and Family

To view a person's photos, you have to find them and then follow them. Their pictures then appear in the photo feed on Instagram's home screen.

Find Facebook Friends

The first place to look for Instagrammers to follow is on another social network—Facebook. Chances are you're already connected to your family and friends on Facebook, so you can quickly and easily use those connections to establish similar connections on Instagram.

1. From within the Instagram app, tap the Profile button to display your profile.

2. Tap the Options (three button or gear) icon to display the Options screen.

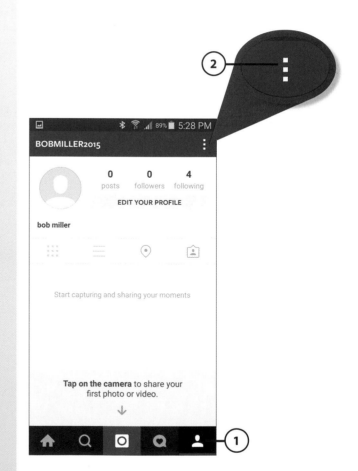

3. In the Follow People section, tap Facebook Friends. This displays a list of your Facebook friends who are also on Instagram.

4. Tap Follow for any friend you wish to follow.

FOLLOW PEOPLE

— 102 Facebook Friends

0 Contacts

Invite Friends

You have 102 Facebook friends on Instagram.

FOLLOW ALL

sfmiller13
Sherry Miller
+ FOLLOW

tofandkristi
Kristi Lee
+ FOLLOW

amyelliott91
Amy Elliott
+ FOLLOW

Find Contacts

You can also let Instagram search the contacts on your phone for people who are also on Instagram. You can then choose to follow selected contacts, if you wish.

1. From within the Instagram app, tap the Profile button to display your profile.

2. Tap the Options (three button or gear) icon to display the Options screen.

3. In the Follow People section, tap Contacts. This displays a list of your contacts who are also on Instagram.

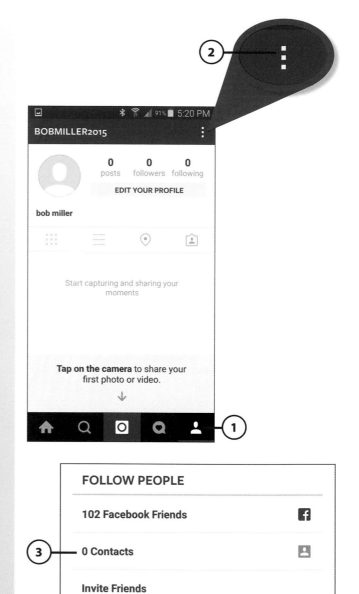

4. Tap Follow for any contact you wish to follow.

Viewing Friends' Pictures

Photos taken by all the friends and contacts you've chosen to follow appear in the feed that displays on the Instagram app's home screen.

1. From within the Instagram app, tap the Home button to display the home screen.

2. Photos from your friends are listed here, newest first. Scroll down to view more.

3. To like a photo, tap the Like (heart) icon.

4. To comment on a photo, tap the Comment icon.

Shooting and Sharing Photos and Videos

You can use the Instagram app to shoot pictures and videos with your smartphone. You can then edit these photos, apply special effect filters, and then share them with your Instagram friends. You can even share your photos to your Facebook or Twitter feeds!

Square Pictures

Unlike your phone's native camera app, Instagram shoots square photos, not widescreen ones—just like your old Polaroids!

Shoot and Share a Photo

1. From within the Instagram app, tap the Photo icon to activate your phone's camera.

2. Make sure that Photo is selected at the bottom of the screen.

3. Tap the Reverse icon to use the front-facing camera to take a selfie.

4. Aim your phone and then tap the big blue round button to take the picture.

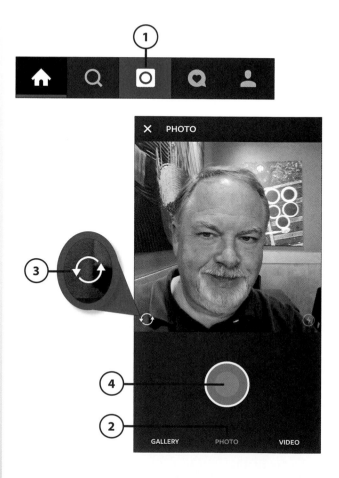

5. You now see a preview of your photo, along with a selection of filters along the bottom of the screen. Tap a filter to apply it to your photo.

6. To adjust the brightness of the photo, tap the Brightness button and then use the onscreen slider to make the picture brighter or darker.

7. Tap the Edit button to further edit your picture—crop the picture, change brightness and contrast, adjust color and saturation, and so forth.

8. Tap the right arrow to display the Share To screen.

9. Tap the Write a Caption field and enter an optional description for this photo.

10. To tag people in this photo, tap Tag People.

11. To also share this photo on Facebook, Twitter, and other social media, tap the social network(s) you want to share to. (You have to previously have linked your Instagram account with these social networks, as described earlier.)

12. Tap the checkmark to share your photo with your Instagram followers and selected social media.

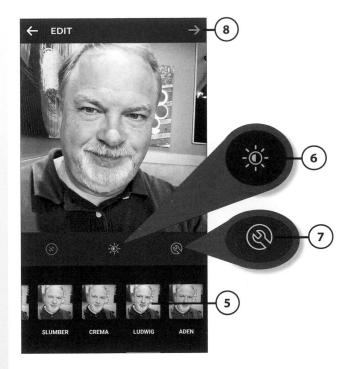

Shoot and Share a Video

Instagram isn't just for still photos. You can also shoot short 15-second videos and share them with your same list of followers and social networks.

1. From within the Instagram app, tap the Photo icon to activate your phone's camera.

2. Tap Video (or the icon of the video camera) at the bottom of the screen.

3. Tap the Reverse icon to use the front-facing camera to shoot the video.

4. Aim your phone and then press and hold the big red round button to start recording.

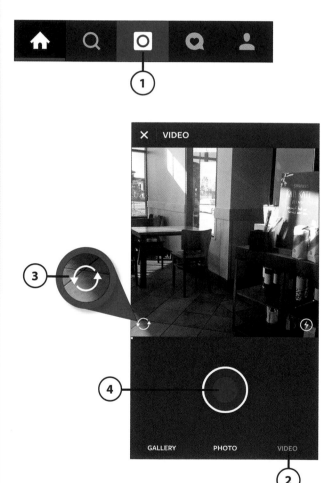

5. Release the button to stop recording. Press it again to resume the current recording.

6. When you're done recording, tap the right arrow or Next.

7. You now see a preview of your video. Tap the screen to begin playback.

8. Tap a filter along the bottom of the screen to apply it to your video.

9. To choose a thumbnail image to represent this video, tap the Choose a Cover Frame icon and make a selection.

10. Tap the right arrow to display the Share To screen.

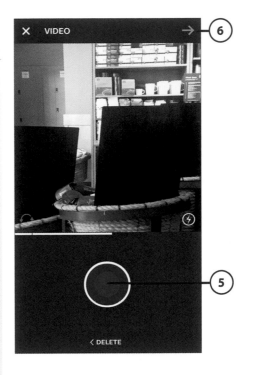

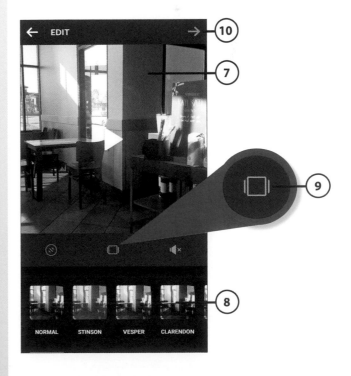

11. Tap the Write a Caption field and enter an optional description for this video.

12. To also share this video on Facebook, Twitter, and other social media, tap the social network(s) you want to share to. (You have to previously have linked your Instagram account with these social networks, as described earlier.)

13. Tap the checkmark to share your video with your Instagram followers and selected social media.

Home   Forums ▾   Meats ▾   Veggies ▾   Desserts ▾   Beverages ▾   Outdoor Cooking ▾   More Foods ▾

Discuss Cooking - Cooking Forums

User Name [User Name]   ☐ Remember Me?
Password [   ]   [Log in]

Register   Cooking Links   Member Photos   FAQ   Community ▾   Calendar   Today's Posts   Search

» Recent Discussions

Title, Username, & Date	Rating	Last Post	Replies	Forum
Eating avocado - are you supposed to mix it with... ChowDownBob 09-18-2015 06:20 AM		Today 11:16 AM by Kayelle	86	Fruit & Nuts
What can I add to my hummous wraps to make more... Cook4984 Today 06:04 AM		Today 11:12 AM by creative	6	General Cooking
Simple Adobo Sauce, for canning: Recipe needed billmac 10-04-2015 08:19 PM		Today 09:48 AM by PrincessFiona60	1	Sauces
Does anyone know a good site to get replacement... larry_stewart Yesterday 11:49 AM		Today 09:33 AM by Bigjim68	9	Cook's Tools

» Discuss Cooking on Facebook

In this chapter, you learn how to interact with like-minded users on special interest message boards.

→ How Message Boards Work

→ Finding Internet Message Boards

→ Reading and Posting to Message Boards

Getting Social on Special Interest Message Boards

If you've got a problem or a question and need help or advice, it's time to go online. While Facebook and similar social networks are great places to interact with friends and family (and maybe get a little general advice), when you have a question about a specific topic, it's time to look for websites that offer special interest message boards.

A *message board* is like a primitive social network, where you hook up with others who share your same specific interests. They work as collections of messages; you post a message, someone else responds to it, and others respond to that. You end up with wide-ranging discussions from interested posters, one message at a time.

How Message Boards Work

Online message boards have been around since before the Internet. They date back to the dial-up Bulletin Board Systems (BBSs) and commercial online services of the 1980s, such as CompuServe and Prodigy. Today, you tend to find them as part of larger websites, typically those devoted to a specific hobby or topic.

Most message boards work in the same fashion. You use your web browser to go to the website, and then click on the link to message boards, discussion forums, or whatever it is these things are called on that site. You may need to register before you can post; most forums will let you read messages without registering, however. (Registering is as simple as clicking the "register" or "sign up" button and then providing whatever information the site asks for—typically your name or nickname, email address, and desired password.)

Boards, Forums, and Groups

What some people call message boards, others call Internet forums, online comments, or discussion groups.

Nutrition	Topics	Posts	Last Post	
Atkins Diet	292	1020	06-19-2015	Join
Blood Type Diet	40	108	03-09-2015	Join
Diabetic Diet	80	291	07-06-2015	Join
Diet Pills	186	662	06-17-2015	Join
Diets and Diet Plans	296	779	06-25-2015	Join
Gluten Free Diet	71	148	05-31-2015	Join
Gout Diet	32	207	05-06-2015	Join
Low-fat Diet	25	103	05-17-2015	Join
Mediterranean Diet	31	61	06-24-2015	Join
Nutrition	1285	3546	07-05-2015	Join
South Beach Diet	21	59	05-12-2015	Join
Vegan Diet	13	28	06-27-2015	Join
Vegetarian Diet	69	393	01-16-2015	Join
Vitamins	850	2835	07-01-2015	Join
Weight Loss	1367	5060	07-05-2015	Join

Message boards

What you see next is typically a variety of different boards, each devoted to a specific topic. Some boards have sub-boards, focusing on a specific aspect of the larger topic. Click to enter the board of your choice, and you see a list of conversations started by other users. These conversations—called *threads*—

revolve around particular subjects and contain messages from multiple users. When you click the subject of a conversation, you see all the messages in that thread, displayed one after another.

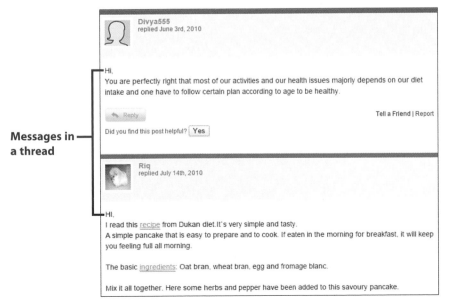

On most boards, the oldest messages in a thread are displayed first, with later messages following in order of posting. So if you want to see the latest messages, you'll have to click to the final page (of a multi-page thread) and then scroll to the bottom.

Messages are typically displayed in self-contained blocks. Each message block contains the poster's name or username, when the message was posted, and often how long the poster has been a member of this particular board. Clicking on a poster's name displays his or her profile information.

When you respond to an existing thread, your message appears at the end. You can also start new threads, by posting a new message with a new subject. Other users will then read your message and respond as they like.

Some boards are moderated, in that the person responsible for that board must approve each new message before it is publicly posted. Other boards don't require this pre-approval, but still have moderators who try to guide the conversations and weed out off-topic posts.

Most boards don't place a limit on the length of your posts, although shorter is always better when you're communicating online. Some boards let users post photos and links to other web pages; others don't. In general, message boards tend to be heavy on text and light on images.

Archived Messages

Whatever messages you and others exchange on a message board are typically stored, or *archived*, for as long as the message board exists. You can browse or search some message boards and find message threads from ten or more years ago. That makes a message board a terrific long-term information resource. (Threads from many message boards pop up when you search Google for those particular subjects.)

Finding Internet Message Boards

Where do you find Internet message boards that might interest you? While there are some sites that offer just message boards, on a variety of topics, the better approach is to look for websites that focus on your favorite topics. Once you find one of these sites, chances are the site offers message boards for its users.

For example, if you're a cat lover, The Cat Site (www.thecatsite.com) connects you with other cat owners and cat lovers to discuss cat health, cat nutrition, cat grooming, and other cat-related issues. (And share cat photos!) That's in addition to the site's regular cat-related articles and content, of course.

If you're into classic cars, you'll find the Antique Automobile Club's website (www.aaca.org) of interest. Not only do you get news and articles about classic automobiles, you'll also find a thriving community of classic car lovers in the site's message forums.

To find these topic-specific websites, fire up your favorite web search engine (Google is my search engine of choice), enter the name of your hobby or interest, and click the search button. Check out the search results for sites that look interesting, and then check out those sites for message boards, discussion forums, or whatever they call their online communities. Chances are the sites you find will have thriving online communities.

You can also check out the more general-interest sites and forums in the table below. These sites have vibrant message forums of particular interest to those of us aged 50 and up.

Online Message Forums for 50+

Forum/ Website	Web Address	Description
AARP Online Community	community.aarp.org	A variety of forums on topics of interest to people aged 50+, including health, work and retirement, money, travel, entertainment and leisure, and technology.
Altdotlife	www.altdotlife.com	A collection of communities revolving around various hobbies and lifestyles, including arts and crafts, cooking, pets, sports, technology, and more.
Buzz50	www.buzz50.com	Forums for over-50s, focusing on social interactions, health, pets, food, travel, and more.
Chow Community	chowhound.chow.com/ boards/	Discussions about cooking, recipes, and more.
Discuss Cooking	www.discusscooking.com	Discussion forums for home chefs, with topics for cookbooks, nutrition, special diets, menu planning, and more.

Forum/ Website	Web Address	Description
Do It Yourself	www.doityourself.com/forum/	A huge number of forums devoted to all manner of DIY projects, including home renovation, gardening, auto repair, interior decorating, and more.
eHealth Forum	www.ehealthforum.com	A great source for health-related questions and answers, with forums for addition and recovery, depression, PTSD, menopause, erectile dysfunction, cholesterol, gout, hemorrhoids, and more.
HealthBoards	www.healthboards.com/boards	All manner of forums focusing on specific health issues, including arthritis, back problems, bone disorders, Alzheimer's disease, epilepsy, Crohn's disease, and more.
HobbyTalk Forums	www.hobbytalk.com/bbs1/	Discussion boards for all manner of hobbies, including collectibles, model kits, R/C cars and planes, and more.
Patient	www.patient.info/forums	Discussion groups targeting specific medical issues, such as depression, anxiety disorders, allergies, diabetes, cancer, and more.
Senior Forums	www.seniorforums.com	Discussions on a variety of topics of interest to older users, including retirement living, health insurance, health, family and relationships, entertainment, hobbies and crafts, and photography.

>>>*Go Further*

COMMENTS SECTIONS

In addition to traditional online message forums, many news and special interest sites allow and encourage readers to comment on the articles on their sites. Commenting on an online article is a bit like commenting on a Facebook post; you read the article, and then type your comments into the following text box. Your comments appear alongside those of other readers; you can then comment on others' comments, and they can comment on yours.

INDYSTAR   HOME   NEWS   SPORTS   LIFE   THING!

JOIN THE CONVERSATION
To find out more about Facebook commenting please read the Conversation Guidelines and FAQs

28 Comments   Sort by   Newest ▾

Add a comment...

Stephen Bailey ·
REALTOR®, Assoc. Broker at F.C. Tucker Co., Inc
I thought the show was an amazing success! I do agree that the elevation in relation to the stage was lacking but regardless of what venue you go to, if you aren't near the front of the stage, you can't see the band very well. The screens were amazing! We were in the bronze section and attempted to move closer but still couldn't see the stage at the front of the bronze section, so we chose the asphalt over the gravel. Logistically, in my experience, the event was handled pretty flawlessly. The speedway could have

Comments on news article

Depending on the nature of the site and its readers, these comments can remain civil and constructive, or devolve into name calling and threats. (It's all too tempting to be an online bully when your comments are anonymous.) To keep the vitriol under control, some sites try to moderate their comments, weeding out those that are too aggressive or personal or just way off-topic. Other sites no longer allow anonymous comments, instead requiring commenters to log in to the site or use their Facebook IDs to comment.

In any case, reading and participating in these comments sections gives you a feel of how people are responding to what's going on in the world today—or just whether or not they agree with a particular article or position. Comments sections are also good places to blow off a little steam, if you don't mind getting burnt by how others respond to what you say. You definitely need a thick skin to participate in some of these sections; it behooves us all, however, to keep things as civil as possible.

Reading and Posting to Message Boards

Every online message board has its own unique look and feel. The processes of reading and posting messages, however, are similar for all sites. For our examples, we'll use the AARP Online Community forums (community.aarp.org), but the steps outlined here should work for most message boards.

Read and Reply to Messages

Once you find a message board or forum in which you're interested, it's a matter of clicking through the layers until you get to the thread you want to read.

1. Click the general category in which you're interested.

2. Click a sub-category to view all the threads within.

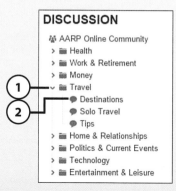

3. The header for each thread displays the subject, number of messages within the thread, original poster, and time/date of the most recent post. Click the subject to view the messages within.

4. The messages in the thread are displayed in order of oldest first. Scroll down the page to view replies to the original message.

5. If there are enough messages in the thread, newer messages are displayed on additional pages. Click the page number to go directly to that page.

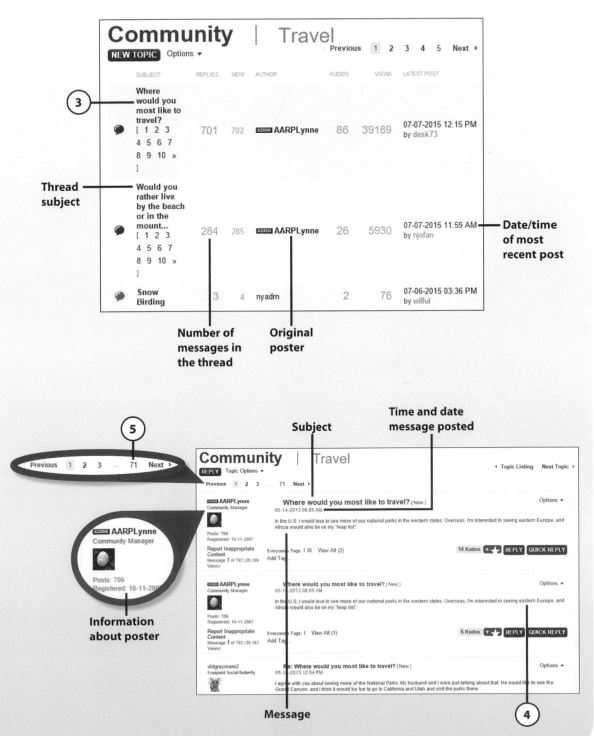

Thread subject

Number of messages in the thread

Original poster

Date/time of most recent post

Time and date message posted

Subject

Information about poster

Message

6. To post a message to this thread, click the Reply button to display the post page or pane.

7. The subject of the thread is already entered into the Subject box. Enter your message into the reply text box.

8. Click the Post button when done. Your message now appears at the end of the thread.

desk73
Info Seeker

Re: Where would you most like to travel? [New]
07-07-2015 12:15 PM

Options ▾

germany, too, for the 500th anniversary of luther

Posts: 1
Registered: 07-24-2012

Report Inappropriate
Content
Message **702** of 702 (5
Views)

Add Tag...

0 Kudos + ▲ ▾ **REPLY** **QUICK REPLY**

6

Subject

Re: Where would you most like to travel?

Body

Rich Text   HTML   Preview

QUOTE

B *I* U S ⚬ <> ☺ 🔗 ▣ ▣ ☰ ☰ Font Family ▾ Font Sizes ▾ A ▾ ⬥

7

CANCEL **POST**

8

Start a New Thread

If you have a new question to ask or a comment to make that doesn't pertain to an existing subject, you can start a new thread to encourage other readers to interact with you.

1. Click the general category in which you're interested.

2. Click the appropriate subcategory.

3. Click the New Topic button to display the post page or pane.

4. Enter the subject of your message into the Subject box.

5. Enter the text of your message into the large text box.

6. Click the Post button. Your message now appears as a new thread on the selected board.

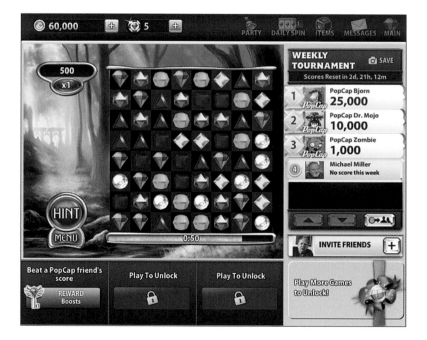

In this chapter, you discover how to have fun on social media with social games.

→ Understanding Social Games
→ Where to Find and Play Social Games
→ Discovering the Most Popular Social Games

Playing Social Games

Why do people aged 50 and older use social media? The number-one reason is to connect with family and friends, of course. Photo sharing is reason number two. But the number-three reason people like you and me use social media may surprise you.

The number-three reason people 50+ use social media is to play games. We're talking social games, where you play along with—and compete against—family, friends, and even strangers.

Who said social media can't be fun?

Understanding Social Games

You've played many different types of games over the years. Physical games, of course, like golf and tennis. Card games, from solitaire to bridge. Board games, from Operation to Monopoly. Casino games, arcade games, trivia games, videogames—the list goes on and on.

Well, all of these games (or variations thereof) are available online. You can play many of these games solo or against a computer. But the fun really gets going when you play against or with other people. Not necessarily someone physically sitting next to you, but rather someone located somewhere else in the world, connecting from his or her computer or smartphone over the Internet.

An online game becomes a *social game* when you play it over a social network, and share aspects of that game with your social media friends. Some social games are single-player games that you play yourself (versus the computer), but then share your scores and accomplishments online. Others are multi-player games that you play against your friends and other social media users. The common factor is that all of these games enable or even require some form of social interaction between players. You're not playing alone.

For example, social card games let you join up online with other players from around the world. You may be sitting at a virtual table playing blackjack with a half-dozen other users, or honing your poker skills with players you've never met in person. The game interaction is facilitated by whichever social network or social gaming site you're using.

Similarly, social board games let you play with and against other players on the same gaming platform. Trivia games let you compare your knowledge against other players on their computers and smartphones. And word games pit you against other online wordsmiths in real time.

However you play them, social games are popular. Very popular. Some of these social games have millions of players, all connecting socially to enhance the game experience. It's a whole new way to have fun—and get social, too.

It's Not All Good

Social Games and Privacy

When you're playing games on Facebook and other social networks, you may run into some privacy issues. That's because many of these social games use your friends list to either obtain information about your friends or send information to them regarding your activity within the game. That's both good and bad.

One of the good things about a social game is that it helps to create a larger community of users by linking you together with your friends. The game might also use your friends' information to provide additional benefit to you. (For example, a game might request that your friends send you in-game items or points.)

The bad thing about a social game is that it makes a lot of personal information public. When you agree to share your information (including your friends list) with the game, you're relinquishing some degree of privacy. You're also betraying the trust of your friends by letting the game access some of their personal information, or post annoying information to their News Feeds. You might be comfortable doing that, and that's fine. But some users don't want to make everything public, and especially don't want to breach their friends' privacy. If that's how you think, then don't sign up for social games that request you share this information. If you don't join in, you won't be jeopardizing your privacy.

Where to Find and Play Social Games

There are lots of places to play social games, both on your computer and on your smartphone or tablet. Many of these platforms offer similar games and similar gaming experiences. Most are free—until you get into in-game purchases, at least. (More on that at the end of this chapter.)

Facebook

Many large social networks offer a variety of social games. Facebook is the big dog here; not only is it the world's largest social network, it also offers the most social games for its users.

If you're a Facebook user (and if you've gotten this far in the book, you probably are), Facebook's Game Center is the place to go when you're looking to play social games.

1. On Facebook's Home page, scroll down the navigation sidebar until you reach the Apps section, and then click Games.

2. This displays the Game Center page. Make sure the Find Games tab is selected.

3. The Home tab, underneath the Find Games tab, displays recommended and popular games in a variety of categories. Scroll down the page to view more games in more categories.

4. Click the Top Charts tab to view the most popular games on Facebook, as well as the most popular games among your friends.

5. Click the Casual tab header to view games in the Puzzle, Board, Trivia & Word, Simulation, Match 3, Runner, Card, and Builders categories.

6. Click the Battle tab header to view games in the Action, Role Playing, Strategy, Card Battle, and Sports categories.

7. Click the Casino tab header to view games in the Slots, Poker & Table, and Bingo categories.

8. Click the name of a game to view more information about the game.

9. Click Play Now to begin playing the game.

AARP Games

The AARP website offers a variety of social games, from Mahjongg and Solitaire to Word Search and Slots. Check them out at **games.aarp.org**.

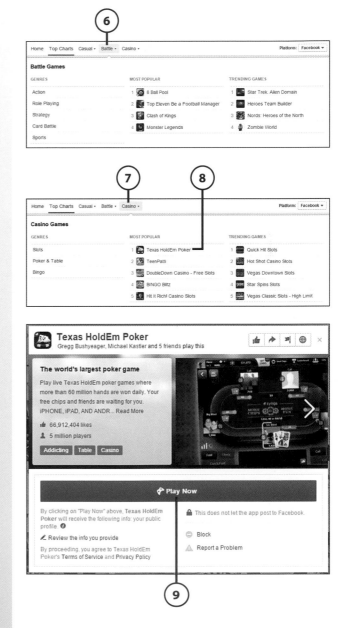

Social Gaming Sites

There are several online gaming sites that offer a good variety of social games, and have developed their own social gaming communities. The most popular of these sites include the following:

- Addicting Games (www.addictinggames.com)
- Agame (www.agame.com)
- Gamesgames.com (www.gamesgames.com)
- Miniclip (www.miniclip.com)
- Pogo (www.pogo.com)
- Youda Games (www.youdagames.com)

Social games on the Pogo website

Mobile Games

There are a ton of social games available for your smartphone. In fact, playing a quick game of Words with Friends or Candy Crush Saga is a great way to spend time when you're stuck in line or waiting for the next appointment at the doctor's office.

Check out your phone's app store to see what games are available. You'll need to download the game to your phone, of course, but then you can start playing by tapping the game's icon on your home screen. Most of these mobile games are free, although many offer in-game purchases that provide additional levels or functionality.

Social games
in the Google
Play app
store

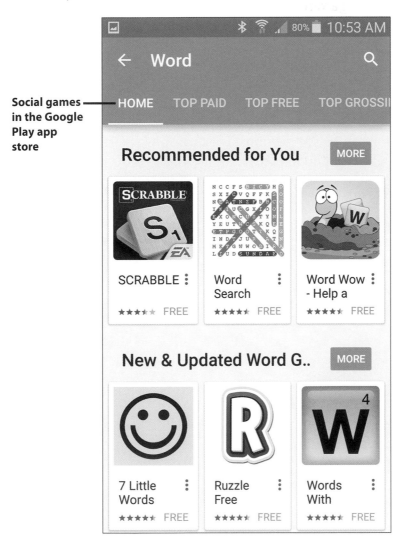

Discovering the Most Popular Social Games

While many games are both timeless and ageless, it's true that there are some games that are more popular with older users than others. Let's take a look at the different social games out there and examine those that have particular appeal to players over the age of 50.

Availability

Not all games are available on all sites or platforms. Look for these or similar games on your platform or social network of choice.

Puzzle and Matching Games

Puzzle and matching games require you to solve some sort of conundrum or match two or more items to score points. For example, with a match-2 game you have to find two matching items; a match-3 game requires you to find three matching items.

Candy Crush Saga

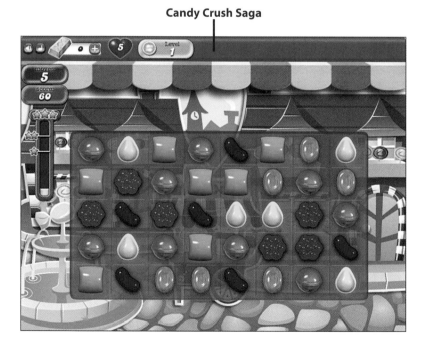

Puzzle Games

Game	Description
Angry Birds Friends	Compete in online tournaments to find all the golden eggs.
Bejeweled and Bejeweled Blitz	Very popular match-3 puzzle games.
Candy Crush Saga	Match-3 game—match three or more colored candies to score.

Game	Description
ConnecToo	Connect every two elements of the same color.
Criminal Case	Solve police cases in this hidden object adventure game.
Farm Heroes Saga	Popular match-3 puzzle game.
Flow Free	Connect matching colors with a pipe.
Jigsaw Puzzles	Construct jigsaw puzzles online.
Pepper Panic Saga	From the makers of Candy Crush Saga, a similar matching puzzle game.
TETRIS	Classic dropping-piece puzzle game.
Threes!	Match-2 puzzle game with sliding tiles.
Two Dots	Connect one dot to another to perform various tasks.

Word Games

Word games are very popular because they're fun to play and require just a good grasp of language.

Words with Friends ——

Word Games

Game	Description
7 Little Words	Solve word puzzles with seven clues and seven mystery words.
Charades!	Play classic party game head-to-head with one or more friends.
Crossword	Play crossword puzzles.
Drop Words	Word-finding puzzle with letters dropping from above.
SCRABBLE	Classic word game; play solo or against Facebook friends.
Scramble with Friends	Challenging word-finding game.
Sudoku	Logic-based number-replacement puzzles.
Word Academy	Find hidden words in a grid.
Word Crack	Find hidden words on the board; play solo or against Facebook friends.
Word Search	Find hidden words on a grid.
Words with Friends	Find hidden words and compete against other players.

Card Games

Card games have always been popular. From solitaire to gin rummy to UNO, there are tons of card games available for social play.

Solitaire Arena

Card Games

Game	Description
Bingo Blitz	Play bingo against friends and family.
Cribbage	Play cribbage in single-player or multi-player mode.
Gin Rummy	Play gin rummy against the computer.
Pyramid Solitaire Saga	A blend of classic solitaire and adventure game.
Skip-Bo	Popular family card game.
Solitaire Arena	Multiple versions in a single game.
UNO & Friends	Play solo or with other players.

Casino Games

Lots of people, young and old, like to hit the local casinos when they can. Now, with casino games online, you don't have to leave your house to play slots or poker or any other Vegas-style games.

Texas HoldEm Poker

Casino Games

Game	Description
Big Fish Casino	Slots.
BlackJack	Play against the computer or in tournaments.
Caesar's Casino	Popular collection of casino games.
Double Down Casino	Variety of casino games, including poker, blackjack, bingo, slots, and more.
GSN Casino	Slots, bingo, video poker, and blackjack.
myVEGAS Slots	Online slot machines.
Slotomania	100 different virtual slot machines.
Slots 777	Vegas-style virtual slot machines, with multi-player slot tournaments.
Texas HoldEm Poker	Play against other players in online poker tournaments.
World Poker Club	Another popular online poker game.
World Series of Poker	Various types of poker plus multi-player online tournaments.
Zynga Poker	Texas hold'em poker; compete against other players online.

Board Games

No doubt you've played more than a few board games in your life. Many of the following board games let you play either against the computer or with family and friends, in real-time online.

Mahjong

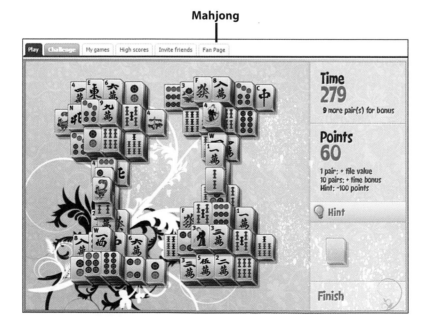

Board Games

Game	Description
Backgammon Live	Play against the computer.
Checkers	Play against the computer or online with other players.
Chess	Play multiple games at the same time against multiple online opponents.
Domino World	Play against the computer or other players online.
Mahjong	Play the classic tile game.
MONOPOLY Millionaires	Fresh take on the classic Monopoly game.
Reversi Free	AKA Othello; 10 difficulty levels.
Stratego	Official version of classic board game.
The Game of Life	Play with up to three friends.
Tic Tac Toe	Play against the computer or another user.
YAHTZEE with Buddies	Play against the computer or other players.

Family Games

Board games are especially good for playing with your children and grandchildren. Most are multi-player games, so you can take turns or play as a team.

Trivia Games

What was the name of Harry Truman's vice president? What TV show did George Clooney star in before *E.R.*? What is the smallest planet in the solar system? If you know the answers to these questions, you'll have lots of fun with the many trivia games available online.

Trivia Crack——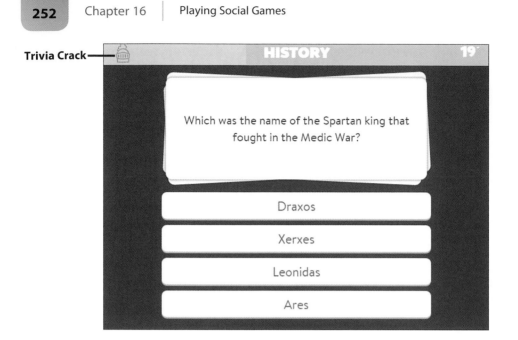

Trivia Games

Game	Description
Brando Mania	Trivia game focusing on well-known (and lesser-known) brands and logos.
Family Feud	Play head-to-head against friends or the larger Family Feud community.
Guess the Song	From 1960s classics to current hits, guess which song you're listening to.
Jeopardy!	Mobile version of the classic TV game show.
Quizoid Pro	Thousands of questions in 17 fields of knowledge.
QuizUp	Multi-player trivia game; join and play in topic communities.
SongPop	Name that tune or artist; play head-to-head with Facebook friends.
Trivia Crack	Play against Facebook friends or random opponents with questions based on Art, Entertainment, Geography, Science, or Sports.
TriviaBurst	Single-player or head-to-head play with a variety of topics and difficulties.
True or False: Quiz Battle	Thousands of true/false questions in 15 categories.

>>>Go Further

GAMES FOR KIDS

Firing up a game on your computer or smartphone is a good way to keep younger children or grandchildren occupied. When they get bored or whiney, just fire up their favorite games and let them play.

When it comes to picking good games for kids, you can't go wrong with arcade games. In particular, Angry Birds (and its many variants, including Bad Piggies) is very popular among the younger set, in part because it's so easy to learn and play.

Other popular arcade-like games for kids include:

- Candy Crush Saga
- Cut the Rope
- Doodle Jump
- Flow Free
- Looney Tunes Dash!
- Minion Rush
- My Tom
- Palace Pets
- PicsArt Kids
- Plants vs. Zombies
- Subway Surfers
- Temple Run
- Where's My Water?

For slightly older kids, Minecraft is extremely popular, almost a phenomenon. Kids from first or second grade on up can spend hours upon hours building and exploring in the Minecraft universe. (Heck, you may find it interesting, too!) Also popular are the various LEGO games, of which there are legions.

Simulation Games

These games let you build your own virtual worlds and then explore and nurture them. They're quite immersive and can eat up a ton of your time!

FarmVille 2

Simulation Games

Game	Description
Dragon City	Build your own magic kingdom, complete with dragons.
FarmVille and FarmVille 2	Create your own 3D virtual farm—one of the most popular games ever on Facebook.
Minecraft	Available on mobile devices or as a freestanding PC game, Minecraft lets users build and explore their own block-like virtual worlds.
TrainStation	Build railroad layouts and your own railroad station.
Zoo World 2	Become a virtual zookeeper by building your own online zoo.

Sports Games

If you're a big sports fan, you may also like to play sports games online. There are lots available, from football and baseball to bowling and pool. There are even fishing and archery games available!

WGT Golf

Sports Games

Game	Description
3D Bowling	Mobile bowling with realistic 3D graphics.
8 Ball Pool	Compete one-on-one or in eight-player tournaments.
Ace Fishing: Wild Catch	Go fishing with friends.
Archery Master 3D	Realistic archery simulation; 4 locations, 20 different types of equipment, and more than 100 levels.
Flick Golf!	Stunning 3D course graphics, multiple courses, and realistic gameplay.
Golf Star	Stunning graphics and true-to-life golf physics.
iFishing	Realistic fishing game, variety of lures available, many freshwater fish to catch.
Madden NFL	Online version of popular football game; customize your roster with players from different teams.
MLB Perfect Inning	Officially licensed product of Major League Baseball; create your own all-star team.

Game	Description
NBA Jam	Play against other local and online players; 2-on-2 basketball action.
PBA Bowling	Dozens of PBA tournaments; bowl against 21 of the best pro bowlers.
TAP Sports Baseball	Create your own fantasy baseball team and play in tournaments and leagues with other players.
WGT Golf	Realistic online golf experience.

Brain Training Games

Playing games can actually be good for your health—your mental health, that is. Some research shows that brain-training games can help improve your memory, focus, comprehension, and more. Some scientists believe that the right games can even slow the symptoms of Alzheimer's and dementia. In any case, there's no harm in doing some brain exercises from time to time—especially if they're fun, too.

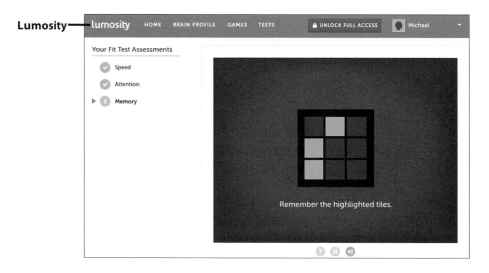

Lumosity

Brain Training Games

Game	Description
Brain Practice	Mathematical calculation game for brain simulation.
Can You Escape	Solve the puzzles to break out of virtual rooms.
Lumosity	Create a personalized training program for memory and attention (available at www.lumosity.com).
Memrise	Game for learning languages and trivia with your friends.
NeuroNation	Memory training to strengthen your memory, improve your attention, increase your intelligence, and make faster decisions.
Sharply—Brain Training Games	Personalized brain training program designed to improve memory, focus, problem solving, mental agility, language skills, and more.

It's Not All Good

In-Game Purchases

Given how many of these social games can be played for free, how do the companies behind the games make money? There are actually two ways.

First, many game companies sell ads within their games. These ads take up valuable screen space, but the hope is that enough people will be interested enough to tap through and actually buy something. Because in-game ads are so annoying, many companies sell ad-free versions of their games, in addition to the free ad-supported versions. You may find it worthwhile to pay a few bucks to get rid of the ads in your favorite games.

Other game companies make money by trying to sell you things within the game. That is, they encourage (or even require) in-game purchases for things like extra in-game currency, more lives, even access to higher levels. In some games, you can't proceed past a certain point without making an in-game purchase. I hate games that require this sort of pay-to-play, especially when my eight-year-old grandson runs into a brick wall that only grandpa's money can fix.

These in-game purchases can also be a little deceiving, especially if you're new to the game. You may think you're just getting more information or moving on naturally, and then later find you've been billed for five or ten or more bucks for an in-game purchase. For this reason, be very careful what you tap when you're playing an online game—you don't want to spend more money than you planned to!

In this chapter, you learn how to video chat with Skype and Google Hangouts.

→ Understanding Video Chatting
→ Video Chatting with Skype
→ Video Chatting with Google Hangouts

Getting Social with Video Chats

Most social media help you connect with friends and family via text messages or photos. That is, you write or upload something and leave it for others to read in their news feeds; it's not real-time interaction.

When you want to get social in person—well, over the Internet, in any case—*video chatting* is the way to go. There are various services available—including Skype and Google Hangouts—that let you use your computer, smartphone, or tablet to chat face-to-face with people in real time. It's like the videophones promised to us in the cartoons and movies of the 1950s and 1960s, except it's here today, and available over the Internet.

Understanding Video Chatting

Not everyone lives close to family and friends. Even if you do have a close-knit local community, you may find yourself missing loved ones when you're traveling. Just because you're far away, however, doesn't mean that you can't stay in touch—on a face-to-face basis.

This is where video chatting (sometimes called *video calling*) comes in. A video call is a face-to-face, real-time chat over the Internet.

To conduct a video call, both you and the person you want to talk to must have webcams built in to or connected to your PCs. In addition, you both must be connected to the Internet for the duration of the call. The video chat uses your device's camera and accompanying microphone to transmit your picture and voice to the other party, over the Internet. You see the person you're talking to via his or her camera and microphone, too. Once connected, all you have to do is start talking.

Naturally, video chat works best if you have a relatively fast and stable Internet connection. On slower connections, the picture might get a little choppy or even freeze from time to time.

Video Chatting via Phone

Because of the high amount of bandwidth used by the video signal, you probably don't want to conduct long video chats on your smartphone over your mobile carrier's data network; those data charges will add up quickly. If you want to use your phone for a video chat, make sure you're connected to the Internet over Wi-Fi.

There are several popular video chatting services available to you today. The two most popular are Skype (owned by Microsoft) and Google Hangouts, which work on Windows and Mac computers, as well as iOS and Android mobile devices. Facebook also offers video chatting from within its social network, and Apple offers its FaceTime video calling for users of iPhones and other Apple devices. All of these services work in much the same fashion, and let you talk via video to the people you love. It's a great way to stay social when you're online.

>>>Go Further
WEBCAMS

Most notebook PCs have webcams built in. You can use your notebook's built-in webcam to make video calls with both Skype and Google Hangouts. Because the webcam includes a built-in microphone, you can also use it to make voice calls.

Webcam connected to a PC

If your PC doesn't have a built-in webcam, you can purchase and connect an external webcam to make video calls. Webcams are manufactured and sold by Logitech and other companies, and connect to your PC via USB. They're inexpensive (as low as $30 or so) and sit on top of your monitor. After you've connected it, just smile into the webcam and start talking.

Video Chatting with Skype

Skype is a service that enables subscribers to connect with one another over the Internet, in real time. You can use Skype to conduct one-on-one text chats, audio conversations, and video chats. (We'll focus on video chats here.)

To use Skype for video calling, you must first download and install the free Skype application, available from www.skype.com or by clicking the Get Skype app on the

Windows Start menu. Once you have the app installed, you can then create your own Skype account. (You can also sign in to Skype with your Microsoft account.)

The basic Skype service is free and lets you make one-on-one voice and video calls to other Skype users. Skype also offers a Premium service, from $4.99/month, which offers the capability of group video chats with up to 10 participants.

Skype for Phone Calls

You can also use Skype to call landline and mobile (non-Skype) phones, for 2.3 cents/minute. Monthly subscriptions are also available if you do a lot of non-Skype calling.

Add a Contact

Before you call someone with Skype, you have to add that person to your Skype contacts list.

1. From within the Skype app, enter into the search box (in the top-left column) the actual name or Skype username of the person you want to locate, and then press Enter or click the Search Skype button.

2. When the search results appear, click the name of the person you want to add.

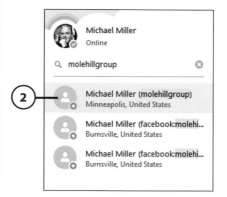

3. Click the Add to Contacts button.

4. You now have to send a contact request to this person. Enter a short message into the text box or accept the default message.

5. Click Send. If the person accepts your request, you'll be added to each other's contact lists.

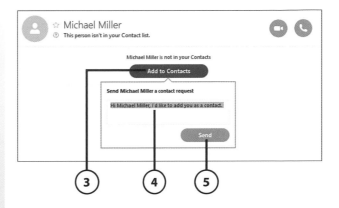

Accepting Contact Requests

Just as you can request someone to be your contact, other people can send contact requests to you. You have the option of accepting or declining any such request. Make sure it's someone you know before you accept.

Make a Video Call

The whole point of Skype is to let you talk to friends and family. You can use Skype to make voice-only calls or to make video calls—which are great for seeing loved ones, face to face.

1. From within the Skype app, go to the Contacts section and click the name of the person you want to call. (People who are online and ready to chat have a solid green dot next to their name.)

2. Click the Video Call (camera) button at the top-right corner of the window.

3. Skype now calls this person. When she answers the call, her live picture appears in the main part of the screen. (Your live picture appears smaller, in the lower-right corner.) Start talking!

4. When you're done talking, click the red "hang up" button to end the call.

Video Chatting with Google Hangouts

Not to be outdone by Microsoft (which owns Skype), tech giant Google also offers video chatting. Google Hangouts are real-time video chats you can participate in either one-on-one or with a group of people. All you need is a Google account—and a webcam on your computer, of course.

Start a Hangout

To start a hangout, point your web browser at **plus.google.com** and, if you're not already signed in, sign in with your Google account.

1. Click the Hangouts (quotes icon) button at the top-right corner of the screen to display the Hangouts panel.

2. All your previous Hangouts are listed here. To resume a previous video call, click that Hangout in the list.

3. To start a new video call, click within the New Conversation box at the top of the panel and enter the name of the person you want to call.

4. Google displays a list of matching names. Click a name to select that person.

5. A new Hangouts window opens on your desktop. Click the Video Call button.

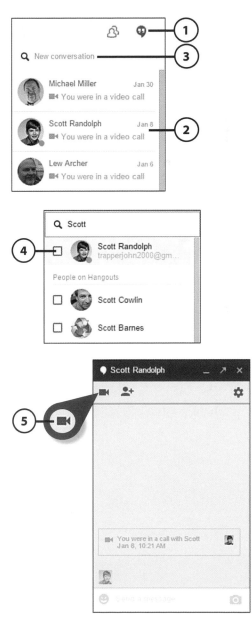

6. When your friend answers the call, his picture appears larger in the Hangout window. Your picture appears smaller, at the bottom. Start chatting.

7. To exit the Hangout, mouse over the window and click the Leave Call button.

Your picture

Create a Group Hangout

Google also lets you create Hangouts with more than two people participating. This is a great way to get your whole family in a single call, even if they're spread all over the country. Group Hangouts are also great for group meetings and other social interactions.

1. Start a Hangout with the first person in the group, as described previously.

2. Mouse over the Hangout window and click the Invite People button to display the Invite pane.

3. When the next dialog box appears, enter the names of the people you want to invite into the Send Invite box.

4. Click the Invite button.

5. When a person answers the invitation, he is automatically added to the Hangout. Whoever is talking at the moment appears in the main window; the other participants appear in smaller windows along the bottom of the screen.

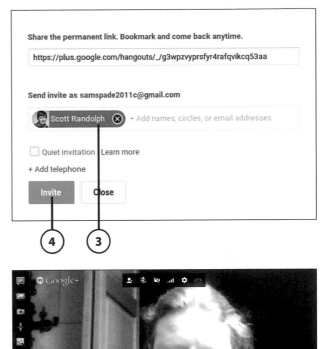

Share the permanent link. Bookmark and come back anytime.

https://plus.google.com/hangouts/_/g3wpzvyprsfyr4rafqvikcq53aa

Send invite as samspade2011c@gmail.com

Scott Randolph ⊗   + Add names, circles, or email addresses

☐ Quiet invitation   Learn more

+ Add telephone

Invite   Close

>>>Go Further

APPLE FACETIME

If you have an iPhone or iPad, and you're talking to another iPhone/iPad user, you can use Apple's FaceTime service for one-on-one video chats. FaceTime works only on Apple devices, so you can't use it with an Android phone or Windows PC. However, it's very easy to use if you have an Apple device.

To conduct a FaceTime call, all you have to do is open the Contacts app and tap a person's name. From that person's contact screen, tap FaceTime. Your phone now calls the other person's phone, and when she answers, you see each other on your respective screens. Start talking until you're done, and then tap the End button.

Search for Friends

Find friends from different parts of your life

Name

Search for someone

Hometown

☐ Indianapolis, Indiana

Enter another city

Current City

☐ Burnsville, Minnesota

Enter another city

High School

☐ Ben Davis High School

Enter another high school

Mutual Friend

☐ Michael Michards

☐ Amy Elliott

☐ Dinah Lance

Enter another name

College or University

☐ Indiana University

Enter another college or unive...

In this chapter, you learn various tips and techniques that help you connect with long-lost friends on social media.

→ Choosing the Right Social Network
→ Searching for Specific Friends
→ Searching for Friends from Your Hometown, School, or Workplace
→ Looking for Mutual Friends
→ Looking for Friends in Facebook Groups

Using Social Media to Find Old Friends

The primary reason most people use social media is to keep in touch with family and friends. I've found Facebook and other social networks to be great places to get back in touch with people I haven't seen in years. I've become newfound "friends" with people I used to work with, old high school buddies, even the next-door neighbor kids I used to play with when I was in grade school. I would have no idea what these people were up to if it wasn't for social media.

How can you use social media to reconnect with old friends, school-mates, and colleagues? It can be a bit of a detective job at times, but there are techniques you can use to find people you haven't heard from in years. Read on to learn more.

Choosing the Right Social Network

When seeking old friends online, the first thing you have to do is choose the right social network. Some are better for finding certain friends than others.

Start with Facebook

Not surprisingly, Facebook should be your first stop in the search for old friends. It's a matter of size; with more than a billion and a half users worldwide, if your friends are online, they're more likely to be on Facebook than on any other social network.

Facebook offers various ways to find people on its site, which we'll discuss later in this chapter. You can search for people by where they live, their hometown, where they went to school, where they used to work, and more. You can also search by first or last name, of course, as well as search for people who are friends of your Facebook friends—and thus are likely to be old friends of yours as well.

That doesn't mean you'll always find the people you're looking for on Facebook. Even with so many users, not everyone in the world is on Facebook. But it's still the best and first place to look.

Look for Business Contacts on LinkedIn

If you're looking for people you used to work with, LinkedIn might be a better choice than Facebook. LinkedIn lets you search for people by company or industry, so you can easily find people who worked at the same companies you did or who operate within the same industry. For that matter, you can find other people who work or worked at a given company and query them about specific people they may known or have worked with.

Participate in Online Message Forums

If you know a particular person has a favorite hobby, you may be able to track that person down through topic-specific websites and message forums. For example, if you went to school with a guy who liked to build model cars and airplanes, start hanging out at The Clubhouse forums (www.theclubhouse1.net). Browse the forums, search the user lists, or even leave a few messages asking about a given person. If you know where to look, you might just find the person you're looking for.

And how do you find topic-specific websites and message forums? That's why we have Google. Just do a search on your topic of choice, then click through the search results until you find an interesting site. Chances are that site will have the message forums you're looking for.

It's Not All Good

Other Social Media—Not So Good

Not every social network is as easy to find people on as are Facebook and LinkedIn. For example, I'd never recommend using Twitter to find old friends; it collects only minimal biographical information about users and really isn't designed to facilitate that kind of social connection. Neither is Pinterest, for the same reasons.

Other social networks simply aren't big enough to be worth your efforts. The Google+ social network, for example, has very few users compared to the larger networks. (Outside of a few niche areas, that is; Google+ is actually an okay place to find younger, tech-savvy people.)

Not that you can't find anybody on these other social media, it's just that your odds are a lot less than when using Facebook or LinkedIn. Feel free to try, but don't be surprised if your efforts are less than successful.

Searching for Specific Friends

Sometimes the most effective friend-finding method is the most direct—just use the search function on any social media site to search for a person by name. And sometimes this will work.

Other times, however, the person may be on that site but not so easily found. Imagine, for example, that you're searching for someone named John Brown. A given site's search results may very well turn up the person you're looking for, but you'd never know because of the other several thousand John Browns listed. When you're searching for someone with a common name, it's easy for that person to hide in plain sight.

For this reason, you may want to fine-tune your search by including other information about that person, as we'll discuss in the next section. Search for John

Brown, but make sure you're filtering by hometown or high school (or whatever) to narrow your results.

You can also include other information in your search query to generate more focused results. Include the person's middle name (if you know it) in the query, along with the person's age or birth date, old email address, names of family members, and so forth. The more precise your query, the more exact the results.

It's especially difficult to find women you used to know, as names get changed along with marital status. Some women have enough forethought to enter their maiden name as their middle name on Facebook and other social media, so the Sara Jensen you used to know might be listed as Sara Jensen McCready, which means her maiden name actually shows up in a Facebook search. Others, however, don't do this—and thus are harder to find.

You can, of course, search for a partial name—searching just for "Sara," for example. What happens next, at least on Facebook, is a little interesting. Facebook returns a list of people named Sara, of course, but puts at the top of this list people who have mutual friends in common with you. That's a nice touch, as it's likely that your old friend has already made a connection with another one of your Facebook friends.

Past that point, you can then display everyone on Facebook with a single first name. But that's going to be a bit unwieldy, unless your friend has a very, very unique name.

Searching for Friends from Your Hometown, School, or Workplace

In the last section, we discussed fine-tuning your search using other details about a person—where she used to live, where she used to go to school, and so on. Some sites make this easier than do others.

Fine-Tune a Facebook Search

When it comes to the variety and quality of search tools offered, Facebook wins the race. Facebook's powerful yet easy to use search tools make it considerably easier to find the people you're looking for. You have the option of filtering your results by a number of key factors, including:

- Hometown
- Current city
- High school
- College or university
- Graduate school
- Employer
- Mutual friends

It's a matter of selecting which of these criteria you're looking for, and then browsing through the results returned by Facebook.

1. Click the Friends button on the Facebook toolbar, and then select Find Friends.

2. Use the Search for Friends section on the right side of the page to conduct your search. To search for someone by name, enter that person's name into the Name box. (If you prefer to search for more than one specific person, leave the Name box blank and use the other search filters.)

3. To look for people who come from your hometown, go to the Hometown section and check your town. (If your hometown isn't listed, enter it into the text box first.)

4. To search for people who live near you now, go to the Current City section and check your city. (If your town or city isn't listed, enter it into the text box first.)

5. To search for people who went to the same high school you did, go to the High School section and check the name of your high school. (If your high school isn't listed, enter it into the text box first.)

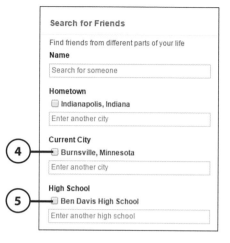

6. To search for people who are already friends with your other Facebook friends, go to the Mutual Friend section and check the names of one or more friends. (If a particular friend isn't listed, enter his or her name into the text box first.)

7. To search for people who went to the same college or university you did, go to the College or University section and check the name of your school. (If your school isn't listed, enter its name into the text box first.)

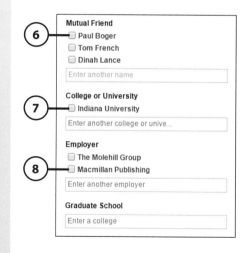

8. To search for people who work or worked for one of your current or former employers, go to the Employer section and check the name of that company. (If a company isn't listed, enter its name into the text box first.)

9. To search for former classmates
who went to the same gradu-
ate school you did, go to the
Graduate School section and
check the name of that school.
(If your grad school isn't listed,
enter its name into the text box
first.)

Multiple Criteria

To further fine-tune your search, select
more than one filter at a time. For
example, you can search for people
who attended your high school and
now live in your current city.

Mutual Friend
☐ Paul Boger
☐ Tom French
☐ Dinah Lance
Enter another name

College or University
☐ Indiana University
Enter another college or unive…

Employer
☐ The Molehill Group
☐ Macmillan Publishing
Enter another employer

Graduate School
9 — Enter a college

Looking for Mutual Friends

Another way to find old friends is to look for people who are friends of your
current friends. That is, when you make someone your friend on Facebook, you
can browse through the list of people who are on his friends list. (Other social
media work similarly.) Chances are you'll find mutual friends on this list—people
that both of you know but you haven't been able to find otherwise.

Find Friends of Facebook Friends

1. Click your friend's name anywhere on the Facebook site, such as in a status update, to display his Timeline page.

2. Click Friends under the person's name to display his Friends page, which lists all of his Facebook friends.

3. When you find a person you'd like to be friends with, click the Add Friend button.

Mutual Friends

If this process doesn't find the person you're looking for, you still may be able to find him by getting in contact with other people who knew that person. Another friend of an old friend might have more current information than you have. Ask questions of any and all mutual friends—when they last saw or talked to this person, whether they have a current email address or phone number, and the like.

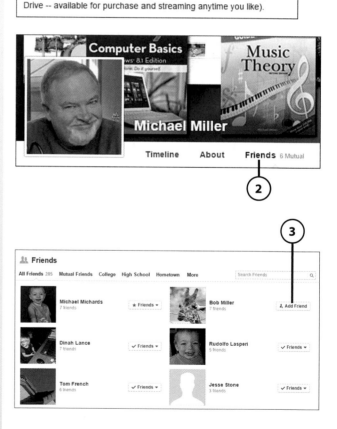

Looking for Friends in Facebook Groups

Another place to search for old friends on Facebook is in Facebook groups. Specifically, look for groups that focus on a particular area of your life—your high school, area of town, place you used to work, general range of years, and so forth. If you're lucky, you may find the person you're looking for as a member of that group. If not, you can always post to the group asking about a given person.

Some examples…

I went to Ben Davis High School in Indianapolis and graduated in 1976. Unfortunately, there's no group for people who graduated my year, but there is a group called Ben Davis High School Class of 1975. That's close enough to contain a lot of people I used to know and has been a boon for reconnecting with former classmates.

There's another high school–focused group I belong to, titled "Ben Davis: Where Is *and/or* Do You Remember." This group is focused solely on finding old classmates over a variety of years. It's a great place for posting questions about people I've long lost touch with.

Looking for friends in a Facebook group

I belong to several other local groups that have proven useful in finding old friends from my youth. There's Ben Davis Alumni Unite!, Growing Up on the Indy Westside, Indy West Side, Old Time Indy's Long Missed Businesses, and more. Some of these groups are more useful than others; some are just fun places to reminisce about days gone by.

I'm sure there are similar groups for your old high school and town. All it takes is a little searching—and then participating in the group to find friends you used to know.

Find a Group

Learn more about finding and participating in Facebook groups in Chapter 7, "Discovering Interesting Groups on Facebook."

>>>Go Further

BEYOND SOCIAL MEDIA

If you're serious about reconnecting with an old friend, don't limit your online search to Facebook and other social media sites. There are other places on the Internet that can help you find specific people.

First, there's Google. It may seem somewhat obvious, but you'd be surprised how many people you can find just by Googling their names. To narrow down the search results, include as much information as possible about that person in your query, and enclose the person's name in quotation marks, like this: "Michael Miller." If you know the person's middle name or initial, include it, too.

Next, there are a number of people search sites on the web. These sites are designed specifically to help you find individuals; most are free, although some charge a slight fee. The most popular of these sites include:

- AnyWho (www.anywho.com)

- PeopleFinder (www.peoplefinder.com)

- Pipl (www.pipl.com)

>>>Go Further

- Spokeo (www.spokeo.com)

- Wink People Search (www.itools.com/tool/wink-people-search)

- ZabaSearch (www.zabasearch.com)

Spokeo

Alumni sites are also good places to track down old schoolmates. Check out Alumni.NET (www.alumni.net), Classmates (www.classmates.com), and Reunion.com (www.reunion.com). If your high school or college has an alumni page or website, check that out as well.

Unfortunately, some of the friends you're looking for may have passed on. Some sites, such as FamilySearch (www.familysearch.org) and Tributes (www.tributes.com), offer free access to the Social Security Death Index, which lists more than 90 million deaths in the United States. You can also check out Legacy.com (www.legacy.com), which offers a database of obituaries published in hundreds of local newspapers.

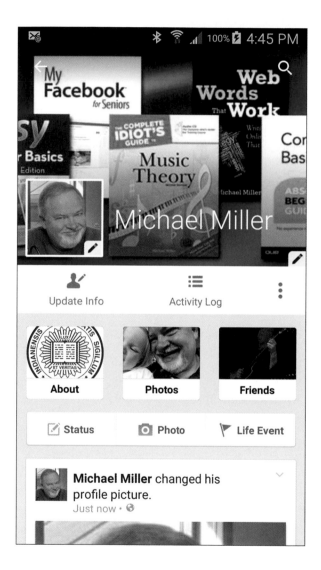

In this chapter, you learn how to use Facebook and other social media on your mobile device.

→ Using Facebook on Your Mobile Device
→ Using LinkedIn on Your Mobile Device
→ Using Pinterest on Your Mobile Device
→ Using Twitter on Your Mobile Device

Using Social Media on Your Smartphone or Tablet

More and more users of every age are connecting to the Internet not via their computers, but with their smartphones and tablets. The old computer-based Internet is increasingly become a mobile Internet, with content and presentation customized for people on the go.

This is also true of social media. All the popular social networks offer mobile apps you can use to connect with on your smartphone or tablet. It's both easy and convenient to check in on your Facebook News Feed or post a status update from your iPhone or Android phone, whether you're at home or on the go.

Using Facebook on Your Mobile Device

Using Facebook on your smartphone or tablet is remarkably easy and convenient. It's easy to post a quick status update or photo when you're out and about, to let friends know what you're doing. It's also nice to be able to use your phone to check your News Feed to see what your friends are up to, especially when you're waiting in line or otherwise occupied.

Facebook offers mobile apps for all major mobile platforms. There are separate apps for:

- iPhone
- iPad (separate from the iPhone app)
- Android (phones and tablets use the same app)
- Windows Phone
- Blackberry

You can download the Facebook app for your device, for free, from your device's app store.

Logging In

The first time you launch any Facebook mobile app, you're prompted to either sign in to an existing account (if you have one) or create a new account. Follow the onscreen instructions to proceed from there.

Use Facebook on Your iPhone

The Facebook app is one of the most popular apps, period, for the iPhone. You can find the Facebook app in Apple's iPhone App Store; just search the store for "Facebook" and then download the app—it's free.

When you first open Facebook's iPhone app, you see the News Feed screen. This is a good starting place for all your Facebook-related activity.

1. Tap the News Feed icon at any time to display the News Feed screen and read posts from friends. Scroll down the screen to view older posts; to refresh the News Feed, pull down from the top of the screen.

2. To view and respond to friend requests, tap the Requests icon.

3. To view notifications from Facebook, tap the Notifications icon.

4. To post a status update, tap Status.

5. To post a photo, tap Photo.

6. To "check in" (post your location only), tap Check In.

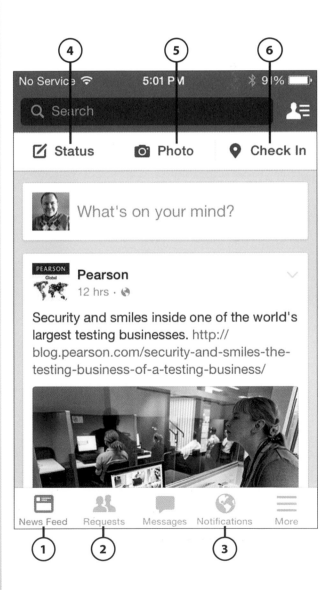

It's Not All Good

Beware Stalkers

Using the Check In feature to broadcast your current location can alert any potential stalkers where to find you—or tell potential burglars that your house is currently empty. Because of the potential dangers, think twice about using this feature.

7. To view your favorite pages and groups, as well as your own Timeline, tap the More icon.

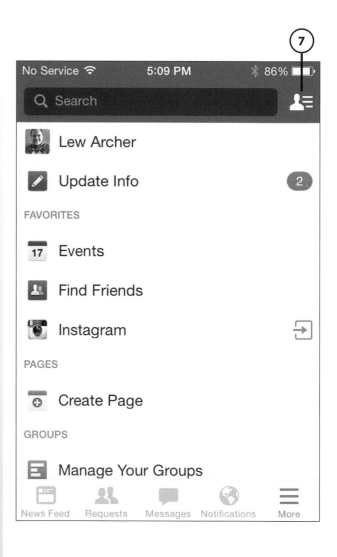

Use Facebook on Your Android Phone

If you use an Android phone or tablet, Facebook has a mobile app for you, too. You can find Facebook's Android app in the Google Play Store; just search the store for "Facebook" and then download the app—it's free.

The Facebook app for Android looks a lot like the Facebook app for iPhone. As with the iPhone version, when you launch the Android app you see the News Feed screen.

1. Tap the News Feed icon at any time to display the News Feed screen and read posts from friends. Scroll down the screen to view older posts; to refresh the News Feed, pull down from the top of the screen.

2. To view and respond to friend requests, tap the Requests icon.

3. To view notifications from Facebook, tap the Notifications icon.

4. To post a status update, tap Status.

5. To post a photo, tap Photo.

6. To "check in" (post your location only), tap Check In.

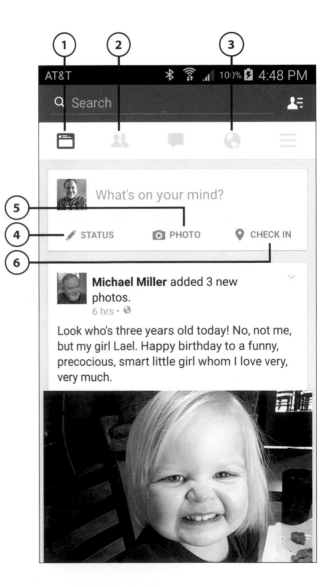

7. To view your favorite pages and groups, as well as your own Timeline, tap the More icon.

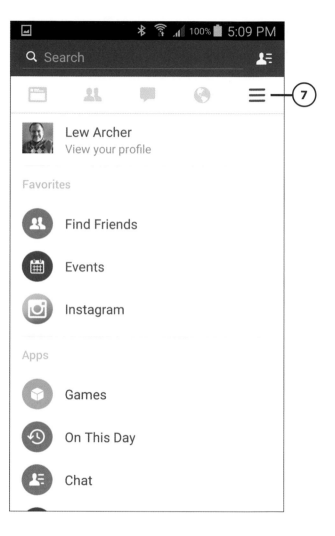

Use Facebook on Your iPad

Facebook offers a separate iPad app that takes advantage of the larger tablet screen. It still does all the same things that the iPhone app does, but with a slightly different layout.

When you first open the Facebook app, you see the News Feed screen. This screen looks different depending on how you're holding your iPad.

1. In landscape mode (held horizontally), you see the News Feed on the left with a Favorites panel on the right side of the screen.

2. In portrait mode (held vertically), you see the normal News Feed with no additional sidebars. To refresh the News Feed, pull down from the top of the screen.

3. To view and respond to friend requests, tap the Requests icon.

4. To view notifications from Facebook, tap the Notifications icon.

5. To post a status update, tap Status.

6. To post a photo, tap Photo.

7. To "check in" (post your location only), tap Check In.

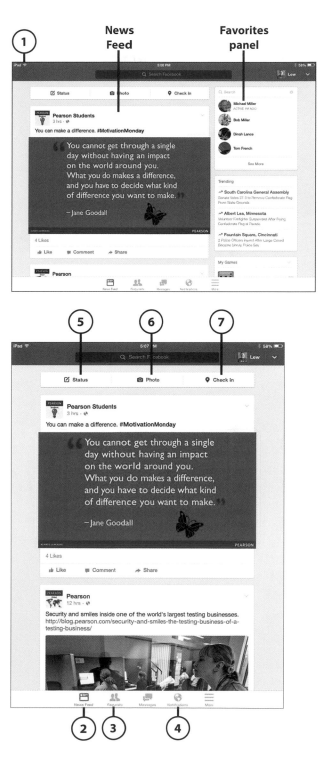

8. To view your favorite pages and groups, tap the More icon.

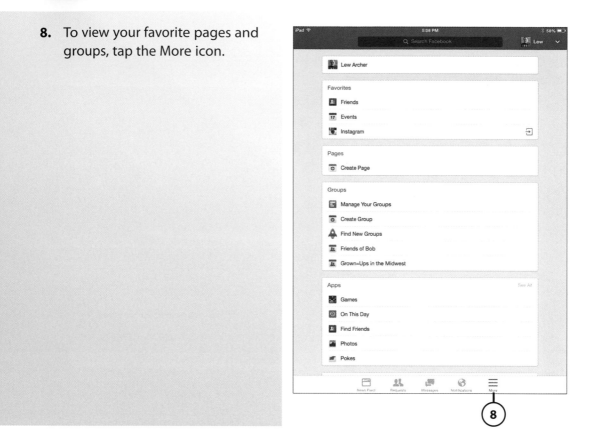

⑧

Using LinkedIn on Your Mobile Device

Like Facebook, LinkedIn offers mobile apps for both iOS and Android devices. (It doesn't offer a separate iPad app, however.) Both apps look and work pretty much the same, and are available for free from your device's app store.

Use LinkedIn on Your Smartphone

For our example, we'll look at the LinkedIn Android app; the iPhone app works pretty much the same.

1. The home screen displays your news feed. Swipe in from the left side of the screen to display the Home panel.

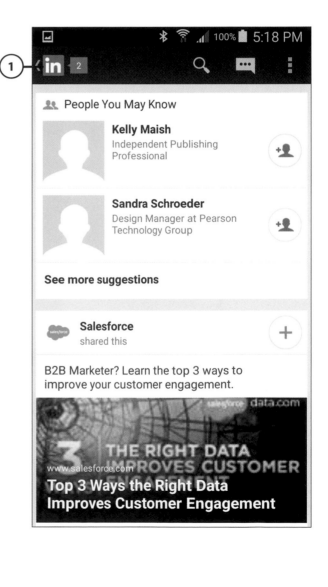

2. Tap Companies to find and follow individual companies.

3. Tap Connections to view people you follow.

4. Tap People You May Know to find other people you may wish to follow.

5. Tap Jobs if you're in the market for a new job.

6. Tap Groups to find and follow topic-specific groups.

7. Tap the messages icon to view and send private messages to other members.

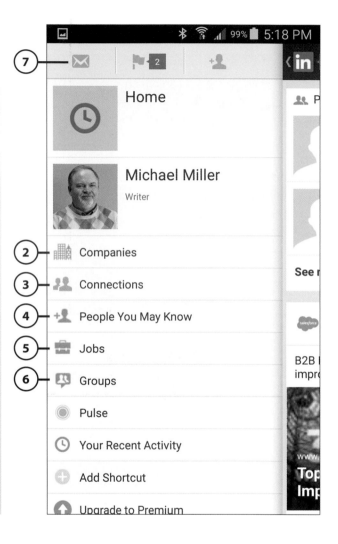

Using Pinterest on Your Mobile Device

Pinterest also offers mobile apps for both iOS and Android devices. You can download the Pinterest app, for free, from your device's app store.

Use Pinterest on Your Smartphone

For our example, we'll look at the Android version of the Pinterest app. The iOS version works much the same way.

1. The Pinterest app launches to your home page, which displays pins you've personally pinned, items pinned by people you follow, and recommended pins from Pinterest. Tap a pin to view it full-screen.

2. To repin this item to one of your boards, tap the Pin It button.

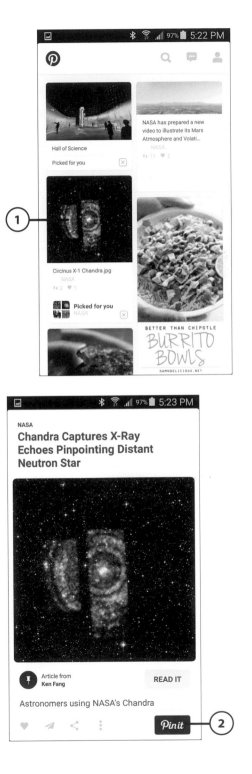

3. Accept or edit the current description of the item.

4. Scroll down and select which board you want to pin the item to. The item is now pinned to that board.

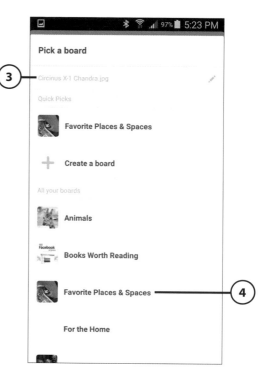

Using Twitter on Your Mobile Device

Last but certainly not least, Twitter offers mobile apps for both the iOS and Android platforms. Like all the other social media discussed here, the Twitter app is completely free and available from your device's app store.

Use Twitter on Your Smartphone

We'll look at Twitter's Android app here. Twitter's iOS app works in much the same fashion.

1. Tap the Twitter icon to display your feed. Tweets from people you follow are listed here.

2. To "star" a tweet you like, tap the star icon.

3. To retweet a tweet (that is, post it to the people who follow you), tap the retweet icon, then tap Retweet.

4. To create a new tweet, tap the New Tweet icon at the bottom of the screen.

5. Use the onscreen keyboard to enter the text for your tweet. Remember to keep it less than 140 characters!

6. To tweet a photo, tap the camera icon, and then select a photo stored on your phone.

7. Tap the Tweet button to post your tweet.

Instagram

The other major social network for older users, Instagram, is purely a mobile medium. Learn more about using Instagram on your smartphone in Chapter 14, "Sharing Photos with Instagram."

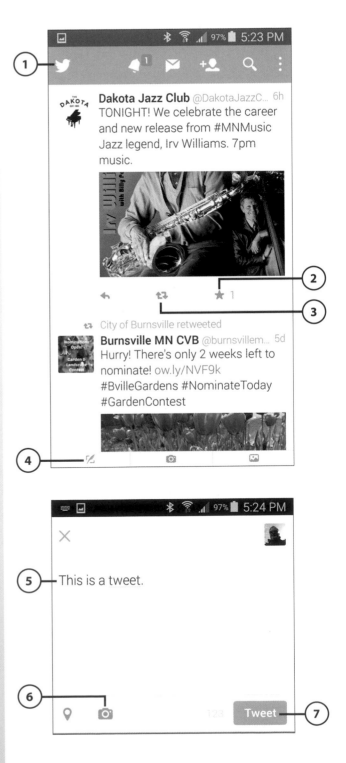

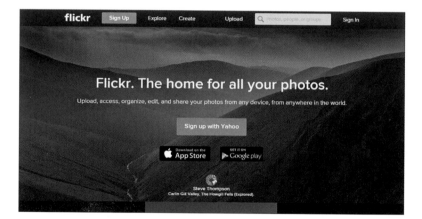

In this chapter, you learn about other social media of interest.

- → Discovering Other Social Networks
- → Discovering Social Bookmarking Services
- → Discovering Media-Sharing Services
- → Discovering Other Microblogging Services
- → Discovering Mobile-Messaging Media
- → Exploring Other Social Websites

Exploring Other Social Media

Facebook, LinkedIn, Pinterest, Instagram, and Twitter are the most popular social media for users aged 50 and up. But they're not the only social media out there. There are lots of other social media, many popular among younger users, that may also be of interest to you.

In this chapter, we briefly examine some of these other social media, many of which are designed specifically for mobile use. Although you might not be interested in some or all of these sites for your own personal use, you might find some of them useful for keeping up with younger members of your family.

Discovering Other Social Networks

Facebook is the largest social network on the Internet today, and LinkedIn is also very popular, at least in the United States. There are other social networks, however, both in the U.S. and abroad, that appeal to specific audiences. Many of these are somewhat country-specific, offering a Facebook-like experience to speakers of a given language.

Google+ social network

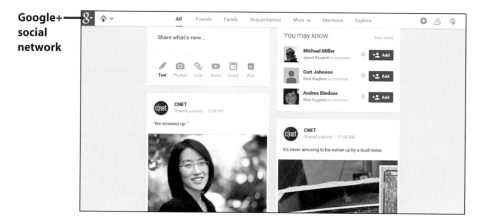

These other social networks include the following:

- **Ask.fm** (www.ask.fm). A social network for high school and college students, where users can ask questions (no matter how embarrassing) of other users, and get frank and hopefully honest answers. Grownups are not particularly welcome on this network.

- **Badoo** (www.badoo.com). A dating-focused social network popular in Latin America, Spain, Italy, and France.

- **Google+** (plus.google.com). This is Google's latest attempt to join the social networking revolution. Despite Google's attempts to tie Google+ into the company's other services and sites, Google+ has not achieved widespread acceptance. Today, Google+ appeals primarily to younger, more technical users. (Programmers and software developers really like it, as do other techie types.) It doesn't attract much of a general audience, however; it's unlikely you'll find many of your friends using Google+.

- **Qzone** (qzone.qq.com). This is the number-two social network worldwide, and the leading social network in China. If you have a lot of friends or relatives in China, it's worth checking out.

- **Renren** (www.renren.com). A social network popular among college students in China. Probably not of much interest for readers of this book.

- **VKontakte** (www.vk.com). Also known as VK, this is the largest social network in Russia. So if you have a lot of Russian friends or family, this is a go-to site.

Discovering Social Bookmarking Services

As you learned in Chapter 4, "Comparing the Most Popular Social Media," social bookmarking services let users share their favorite web pages, websites, online articles, videos, and the like. Instead of sharing an entire item, a user bookmarks the page on which the item appears and then shares that bookmark with interested parties on the social bookmarking site.

Social News

Social bookmarking sites are sometimes called *social news sites*, as news articles tend to be among the most bookmarked and shared items.

With most social bookmarking services, a user clicks a button for that service on a given web page or on a toolbar installed in the user's web browser. Clicking the button saves a bookmark or reference to that page on the social bookmarking site. Bookmarks are typically saved in a user's personal folder on the bookmarking site, but are also made public for other users to reference from the site.

Reddit social bookmarking service

When you bookmark a page or article, you add descriptive keywords to the bookmark. When you or other users search the social bookmarking site by keyword, the site then displays all bookmarks that match the keyword query.

In addition, some social bookmarking sites organize their bookmarks by category, such as technology or entertainment, enabling users to browse bookmarks in this fashion. These sites often offer web feeds for their lists of bookmarks, which enables users to subscribe to particular lists and be automatically notified of new bookmarks as they're added.

While there are dozens of active social bookmarking services today, the following are the most popular among U.S. users:

- **Delicious** (www.delicious.com). Unlike some other social networking services, Delicious makes all of its bookmarks public by default. Delicious features a hotlist of the most popular bookmarked pages and articles on its home page, and offers Really Simple Syndication (RSS) feeds of bookmarks by tag.

- **Digg** (www.digg.com). At one point, Digg was the largest and most popular social bookmarking site. Following several years of dwindling use, however, the site was sold (in 2012), and the new owners relaunched the site, essentially from scratch. The "new" Digg has a much smaller user base than did the original site during its heyday.

- **Reddit** (www.reddit.com). Reddit is the most popular and fastest-growing social bookmarking site today, attracting a primarily young, male, tech-savvy audience; many of the most popular topics on the site are technology-related. Reddit offers "up" and "down" voting on bookmarks, as well as discussion areas where users can discuss shared items. The reddit site is built around a series of topic-oriented communities called *subreddits*, each with its own purpose, standards, and moderator. While there are thousands of existing subreddits, any user can create a new subreddit as the topic demands.

- **StumbleUpon** (www.stumbleupon.com). The first true social bookmarking service, StumbleUpon augments its bookmarks and thumbs-up, thumbs-down ratings with a personalized recommendation engine that suggests web pages to visit based on a user's ratings of previous pages. To view a list of suggested pages, users click the Stumble! button on the site's home page or toolbar.

RSS Feeds

Most blogs, news-oriented websites, and some social bookmarking services offer *feeds* of their newest content, which are then "fed" to newsreader applications and websites. These news feeds help interested users keep up-to-date with the latest postings.

Discovering Media-Sharing Services

Aside from Pinterest and Instagram, there are a number of media-sharing services online. Many are mobile-only networks; most have mobile apps that let you snap photos or shoot videos on your mobile phone, and then share them online with your friends and followers.

YouTube video-sharing service

The top photo- and video-sharing social networks today include the following:

- **Flickr** (www.flickr.com). Owned by Yahoo!, Flickr is the largest photo-sharing community on the web, with more than 80 million users. Because of its large user base, Flickr offers the most opportunities for social networking. Basic membership is free, although paid memberships are available that let users store and share a larger number of photos online. Flickr displays a user's stream of photos (literally, a *photostream*) on its main page; you can then search for photos by keyword or browse the most recent uploads, and then share the photos you like with your friends.

- **Fotki** (www.fotki.com). Like Flickr, Fotki is a free photo-sharing community. You can easily search Fotki for photos by keyword or from a specific member.

- **Fotolog** (www.fotolog.com). Lets users share digital photos via online photo diaries and photoblogs.

- **Photobucket** (www.photobucket.com). Similar to Fotki and Flickr, Photobucket is a free photo-sharing community that lets you search for photos by keyword.

- **Picasa Web Albums** (picasaweb.google.com). Owned by Google, Picasa Web Albums lets you upload your photos into albums and specify who can view your albums. You can also perform simple keyword searches for photos from other users.

- **Snapchat** (www.snapchat.com). A mobile social network that lets users shoot photos and short videos, and then share them with other friends on their smartphones. Unlike other social networks, there is no archived trace of users' activity; shared photos and videos "disappear" 10 seconds after viewing. Very popular among younger users.

- **Vimeo** (www.vimeo.com). A video-sharing network, similar to YouTube, but with an additional focus toward business users.

- **Vine** (www.vine.co). A mobile social network that lets users shoot and share short (six-second) looping videos from their mobile phones. Very popular among younger users.

- **YouTube** (www.youtube.com). Owned by Google, YouTube describes itself as "the world's most popular online video community." It is a site that enables users to upload their own digital videos and share those videos with other users. YouTube offers an interesting and ever-changing mix of amateur and professionally-produced videos that are easily sharable with friends and followers.

Discovering Other Microblogging Services

A *microblog* is similar to a traditional blog, in that it is a way for creators to broadcast their views and content to a wide, web-based audience. It differs from a traditional blog, however, in that each *micropost* is typically much shorter than a traditional blog post—in some instances, only a sentence or two. Some microblogs consist solely of pictures or videos, with little or no accompanying text. The result is a medium best suited for immediate and direct proclamations, rather than long and involved musings.

Tumblr
microblogging
service

As you've learned, Twitter is the Internet's most popular microblogging service. But it's not the only one. If you're into reading very short blog posts from other users, or making such posts yourself and then sharing them, check out the following:

- **Plurk** (www.plurk.com). Plurk is the most Twitter-like of these competing microblogging services. Users post short (210-character) updates, called plurks, which are shared on followers' timelines.

- **Sina Weibo** (www.wiebo.com). A popular microblogging service in China.

- **Tencent Weibo** (t.qq.com). Another popular Chinese microblogging service.

- **Tumblr** (www.tumblr.com). The number-two microblogging service in the U.S., Tumblr is subtly different from Twitter, offering true microblogs, not just a stream of unrelated messages. All of a user's posts are collected on his Tumblr blog page; users can post any combination of text, photo, video, and audio content.

Discovering Mobile-Messaging Media

As more and more older people gravitate toward Facebook, they're driving away younger users. (How hip can a social network be when your grandparents are using it?) Where are all these younger users going?

To some degree, they're scattering, using a mix of Instagram, Snapchat, Twitter, and similar media. But they're also moving toward dedicated mobile-messaging services—social networks that let users send and receive text messages and photos to and from each other's phones. These services are kind of like text messaging on steroids, with the added ability to conference in multiple friends for group chats.

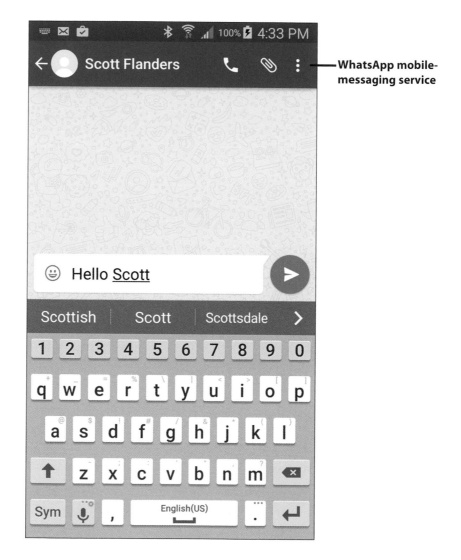

WhatsApp mobile-messaging service

The most popular of these mobile-messaging apps include the following:

- **Kik Messenger** (www.kik.com). This smartphone app lets users send text and photo messages to their friends and families. It's free, has no message or character limits, and is very, very popular among the teen set. Messages can be one-to-one or sent to groups of friends.

- **Oovoo** (www.oovoo.com). This is a video-messaging app with serious group-messaging options. The app is free and offers your choice of text, voice, and video messaging. Oovoo's big attraction is its group-chatting feature. Users can participate in group chats—kind of like Google Hangouts—with up to a dozen friends. It's not unusual for teens to start a Oovoo chat with a handful of classmates and keep it open while they do their homework for the evening. (Or just watch TV. Or whatever.)

- **Viber** (www.viber.com). Messaging app for smartphones that enables users to send and receive text, image, video, and audio messages.

- **WeChat** (www.wechat.com). The largest text and voice-messaging app in China.

- **WhatsApp** (www.whatsapp.com). WhatsApp is a lot like Kik, but with text, audio, video, and photo messaging. People use their smartphones to send messages to single recipients or groups of friends, with free unlimited messaging. In other words, it's a great alternative for kids who push up against the limits of the phone company's standard text-messaging plans.

- **Yik Yak** (www.yikyakapp.com).This is a location-aware social networking app. Users post short, anonymous text comments, which then get distributed to the 500 Yik Yak users in closest physical proximity—typically within a mile or two of the poster. This makes Yik Yak particularly appealing to school kids; whatever they post gets seen immediately by other users on campus, or even in the same classroom.

Exploring Other Social Websites

There's a whole universe of social media sites and services that we haven't had time to explore in this book. Some are appealing to older users, others are more targeted toward the younger generation.

Goodreads,
a social
website for
book lovers

If you have the time and the interest, you can check out some of these social media sites. Here's a short list:

- **BlackPlanet** (www.blackplanet.com), targeting the African-American community

- **Buzznet** (www.buzznet.com), focusing on music and pop culture

- **Care2** (www.care2.com), an online community focusing on healthy and green living, especially targeting social activists

- **CaringBridge** (www.caringbridge.org), a nonprofit, charitable network of free websites for people facing serious medical treatment

- **Classmates.com** (www.classmates.com), tasked with helping people find old classmates; also focuses on "nostalgic content" such as high school yearbooks, class reunion planning, and the like

- **DeviantArt** (www.deviantart.com), a community of artists and art lovers

- **Flixter** (www.flixter.com), focusing on movies

- **Foursquare** (www.foursquare.com), a location-based social presence network, to help you connect with other nearby users

- **Goodreads** (www.goodreads.com), a website and social community for book lovers and avid readers

- **LiveJournal** (www.livejournal.com), a social network consisting of user-written journals and blogs

- **Tagged** (www.tagged.com), a service designed to help users meet new people

- **Viadeo** (www.viadeo.com), used by business professionals around the world

Glossary

blog   Short for *web log*, a shared online journal consisting of entries from the site's owner or creator.

board   On Pinterest, an online corkboard, where images and videos can be virtually pinned.

bookmark   A means of identifying a web page for future viewing or sharing with other users.

bulletin board system (BBS)   A private online discussion forum, typically hosted on a single computer and accessed by other computers via a dial-up telephone connection. BBSs were popular before the advent of the Internet.

connection   On LinkedIn, a professional contact or "friend."

cyberbullying   A form of personal intimidation conducted using social media, mobile phones, and other electronic technologies. Cyberbullies make deliberate and repeated posts that seek to embarrass, humiliate, manipulate, or harm the recipient.

dial-up computer network   A commercial online service that connects multiple computers via a dial-up telephone connection and offers various community-based features, such as email and message forums. These early online networks, such as CompuServe, Prodigy, and America Online, typically charged some combination of monthly and hourly access fees.

discussion forum   See *message board*

event   On Facebook, a scheduled activity, much like an item on a personal schedule.

Facebook   The largest social networking site on the web, Facebook was launched in 2004 and currently has more than 1.5 billion users.

flame war   A heated or hostile interaction between two or more people in an online forum.

Flickr   The web's largest photo-sharing site, with features for both amateur and professional photographers.

follow   How you connect to other users on various social media sites. When you follow a person, his or her new posts display in your feed or on your home page.

friend   On a social network, another user with whom you communicate. Most social networks enable you to create lists of friends, who are authorized to view your posts, photographs, and other information.

friending   The act of adding someone to a social network friends list.

Friendster   One of the earliest social networking websites. Launched in March 2002, Friendster (www.friendster.com) enjoyed a brief period of success before being supplanted by Facebook and other modern social media.

Goodreads   A website and social community for book lovers and avid readers.

Google Hangouts   A popular video chatting service offered by Google.

Google+   Introduced in June 2011, Google+ is Google's social network.

group   On Facebook, a topic- or activity-oriented community page where people interested in a given topic or activity can view information and photos, exchange messages, and engage in online discussions about that topic or activity. On the LinkedIn site, it's a user forum dedicated to a topic of mutual interest.

hashtag   A means of indicating an important word in a tweet, similar to identifying a keyword. Hashtags start with a hash character (#) followed by a word or phrase with no spaces. (Hashtags can also be used on other sites, such as Instagram and Pinterest.)

identity theft   A form of fraud in which one person pretends to be someone else, typically by stealing personal information, such as a bank number, credit card number, or Social Security number. The intent of identity theft is often to steal money or obtain other benefits.

Instagram   A photo-sharing app and social network that enables smartphone users to shoot and share pictures and short videos.

instant messaging   A means of conducting a one-to-one text communication in real time over the Internet or a closed computer network.

keyword   A word in a search query that describes something you're looking for.

LinkedIn   A social network for business professionals.

malware   Short for *malicious software*, any computer program designed to infiltrate or damage an infected computer. Computer viruses and spyware are the two most common types of malware.

media-sharing network   A social network that enables the sharing of various types of media files (photographs, videos, and music) with other users.

message board   An online space where users can read and post messages on a given topic. Many websites offer message forums for their members.

microblogging service   A web-based service, such as Twitter or Tumblr, that enables users to post short messages to interested followers in a blog-like format.

micropost   A short post to a microblogging site.

mobile app   An application for a smartphone or tablet that performs a specific function. Most social networks offer mobile apps for major mobile platforms.

mobile messaging media   Mobile apps that enable person-to-person text, photo, and/or video messaging in a social setting.

MySpace   Launched in 2003, MySpace (www.myspace.com) was the leading social network site until the rise of Facebook.

news feed   On a social network, a collection of posts or status updates from a person's friends.

Page   On Facebook, a page for fans or followers of an entertainer, celebrity, company, or product.

Pages Feed   A special News Feed consisting only of status updates from those Facebook Pages you've liked.

photo album   On Facebook, a collection of digital photographs or videos organized by some underlying theme or topic.

photo-sharing site   A website where users can upload, store, and share digital photographs with other users.

photostream   On Flickr, a feed of photos from a given user.

Picasa Web Albums   Google's online photo storage/sharing service.

pin   An item that has been virtually attached to a Pinterest board. The act of placing a pin onto a Pinterest board is called *pinning*.

Pinterest   Launched in March 2010, a visual social network. Users "pin" interesting images on virtual boards, which are then shared with online friends and followers.

profile   A collection of personal information, including photos, contact information, likes and dislikes, and recent posts for a member of a social networking site. The profile page (on Facebook, presented as a "timeline" of activity) serves as a member's home page on a social networking site.

reddit   A social bookmarking service, launched in 2005, that enables users to submit web pages and other content and then rate that content with "up" and "down" voting.

repin   The act of pinning an item that another user has previously pinned to the Pinterest site.

retweet   A tweet forwarded to other Twitter users.

RSS feed   A format used to automatically publish or syndicate website updates. Users subscribe to a site's feed and then receive updates to that site, typically through some sort of news reader software or website. (RSS alternately stands for Rich Site Summary or Really Simple Syndication.)

Skype   One of the most popular video chatting services, owned by Microsoft.

smartphone   A mobile phone with advanced computer-like capability, typically including Internet access and the ability to run task-specific apps.

Snapchat   A mobile social network that enables the sharing of pictures and videos that are automatically erased ten seconds after viewing.

social bookmarking service   A web-based service, such as reddit and StumbleUpon, that helps users bookmark and share popular websites, web pages, and articles.

social game   A game played on a social network or online gaming site between users of that site.

social media   Websites, services, and platforms that people use to share experiences and opinions with each other. The most common social media include social networks, social bookmarking services, and microblogs.

social network   A website, such as Facebook or LinkedIn, where users can form communities with like-minded people and share details of their lives with friends, family, fellow students, and co-workers.

spyware   A malicious software program that obtains information from a user's computer without the user's knowledge or consent.

status update   A short post from a member of a social networking site, conveying the user's current thoughts, actions, and such.

StumbleUpon   Another popular social bookmarking service, which augments its bookmarks and thumbs-up, thumbs-down ratings with a personalized recommendation engine that suggests web pages to visit based on a user's ratings of previous pages.

subreddit   A topic-oriented community on the reddit site.

tag   The act of identifying a friend in a status update or uploaded photo.

tumblelogs   *Microblogs* were initially called tumblelogs (or tumbleblogs), which is the genesis of Tumblr's name.

Tumblr   A microblogging service, launched in 2007, which enables users to post short text or image messages to their own "tumbleblogs," which other users can then follow online.

tweet A short, 140-character post on the Twitter social media network. Also used as a verb, "to tweet."

Tweeter Someone who tweets on Twitter, also known as a Twitterer.

Twitter A popular microblogging service, launched in 2006, where users post short text messages ("tweets") of no more than 140 characters, which other users can then follow.

unfollow To no longer follow a given person on a social network.

video chat A real-time, face-to-face chat between two people, using their computers or smartphones and built-in cameras or webcams.

Vine A mobile-only, media-sharing service that enables users to post short (six-second maximum) videos from their mobile devices.

viral Achieving immense popularity via word of mouth on the Internet.

website community A website designed to promote a community around a specific topic. Most website communities feature topic-specific articles and other content, along with discussion boards, chat rooms, and the like.

WhatsApp One of the most popular mobile messaging services.

YouTube The Internet's largest video-sharing community, where members upload and view millions of video files each day.

Index

REGISTER THIS PRODUCT
SAVE 35%*
ON YOUR NEXT PURCHASE!

How to Register Your Product

- Go to quepublishing.com/register
- Sign in or create an account
- Enter ISBN: 10- or 13-digit ISBN that appears on the back cover of your product

Benefits of Registering

- Ability to download product updates
- Access to bonus chapters and workshop files
- A 35% coupon to be used on your next purchase – valid for 30 days
  To obtain your coupon, click on "Manage Codes" in the right column of your Account page
- Receive special offers on new editions and related Que products

Please note that the benefits for registering may vary by product. Benefits will be listed on your Account page under Registered Products.

We value and respect your privacy. Your email address will not be sold to any third party company.

* 35% discount code presented after product registration is valid on most print books, eBooks, and full-course videos sold on QuePublishing.com. Discount may not be combined with any other offer and is not redeemable for cash. Discount code expires after 30 days from the time of product registration. Offer subject to change.

quepublishing.com